CAROL ORSBORN

INNER
EXCELLENCE

SPIRITUAL
PRINCIPLES OF
LIFE-DRIVEN
BUSINESS

NEW WORLD LIBRARY
San Rafael, California

© 1992 Carol Orsborn

Published by New World Library
58 Paul Drive
San Rafael, CA 94903

Cover design: Greg Wittrock
Typography: T·H Typecast, Inc.

Library of Congress Cataloging-in-Publication Data

Orsborn, Carol.
    Inner excellence : spiritual principles of life-driven business /
by Carol Orsborn.
      p. cm.
    Includes bibliographical references.
    ISBN 0-931432-92-8
    1. Success in business. 2. Creative ability in business.
3. Excellence. 4. Self-actualization (Psychology) 5. Self
-realization. 6. Stress management. I. Title.
HF5386.069 1992   91-38491
650.1–dc20   CIP

First Printing, April 1992
Printed in the U.S.A. on acid-free paper
10 9 8 7 6 5 4 3 2 1

To my partner in business and in life, Dan Orsborn
And to our beloved children, Grant and Jody

AUTHOR'S NOTE

Former and current clients of The Orsborn Group Public Relations, Inc., and subscribers to "Inner Excellence: The Bulletin of Business and Spirituality" have contributed case histories and anecdotal support for the principles shared in this book. When requested, I have honored their desire for anonymity by changing personal and company names and fictionalizing details.

ACKNOWLEDGMENTS

With great respect I acknowledge my visionary editor Leslie Keenan and the entire staff of New World Library, and Munro Magruder of Business Media Resources, who demonstrate day in and out that the principles I share in this book can work even in the demanding world of publishing.

Offering support and encouragement early on were Robert D. Haas, Chairman and Chief Executive Officer of Levi Strauss & Co., Sandra Dijkstra and members of our advisory board, Louis B. Barnes, D.B.A., Professor of Organizational Behavior at the Graduate School of Business Administration, Harvard University and Dr. Kenneth R. Pelletier, Director, Corporate Health Program, Stanford Center for Research in Disease Prevention.

In gratitude for their courage, I acknowledge Dan Orsborn and the staff of The Orsborn Group Public Relations, Inc. and of Inner Excellence, who have joined me in turning our company into a living laboratory in which to test the practical application of alternative philosophies in a mainstream business environment.

Finally, I am grateful to six fellow travellers who have taught me—with compassion and wisdom—that the cost of integrity is always worth paying: my friends Catherine Holmes, Lisha Gray and Catherine Hand, my spiritual mentors Maggie Bell and Robin Tribble, Master of Divinity. And above all, my agent and confidant Patti Breitman who has graced me with her enormous generosity of spirit, walking with me from inception to publication of this book and beyond, every step of the way.

TABLE OF CONTENTS

INTRODUCTION:
YOU CAN WORK LESS AND ACHIEVE MORE

OR YEARS, I suffered the recurring nightmare that I was danc-
ing on a stage in front of a packed audience – and had forgot-
ten how to do the steps. Little did I know that one spring
day in 1988 I was to suffer – in real life – as terrible a fate. On
that balmy day, I was presenting a speech before an audience of
my peers – nearly one thousand businessmen and women who had
flocked to an auditorium in a major southern city to hear my ideas
about ambition and success.

The speech was not new. I had presented it an average of twice
a month to audiences throughout the country ever since word of
my organization Superwomen's Anonymous broke prominently in
the *New York Times*. The organization, soon expanded to include
men under our current name, Overachievers Anonymous, was the
perfect organization for those who were already overly committed.

The group was founded on the platform of no meetings, no classes, no fundraisers. In fact, we wouldn't do anything.

People signed up in droves. Nearly 5000 businesspeople sent in for membership cards, vowing to consult our organization's motto "Enough Is Enough" before saying yes to anything. Thirty thousand bought our handbook. The organization was my upbeat way of explaining personal decisions my husband and partner, Dan, and I had made concerning the role of ambition and success in our life.

The road that led to that fateful speech began several years before – the day Dan and I signed the mortgage papers on the house of our dreams. Along with many of our generation, the post-World War II boom babies, we had bought the myth that we could have it all. On top of our sixty-hour work weeks spent running our growing public relations agency, The Orsborn Group Public Relations, Inc., we added one child – and then another. Fulfilling our expectation that our hard work and goodness would be rewarded, we pictured the idyllic suburban setting for our growing family. There would be children romping happily on green lawns. A dog would be napping in front of the fireplace. And Dan and myself? While the ink was still wet on the mortgage papers, I had the sinking realization that we would be at the office every day of the week until nine or ten P.M. to pay off this dream.

The youthful ambition that had fueled our race to the finish line was leaving us just when we needed it most. For as long as we could remember, we'd been using sheer willpower and effort to keep the structure intact. Our business won our industry's highest award; but Dan and I shared the feeling that our work seemed to take more from us than it gave back. The more our business expanded, the more the employees demanded of us. We were consumed by the struggle to get new clients, and pushing to keep the staff functioning enough to pay for our increasing overhead. We'd be lucky to break even, let alone turn a profit.

How could we ask our staff to try any harder, work longer or strive for more excellence? We were already at the limit. And it was becoming obvious to us that the harder we worked, the farther behind we were falling. There was no inspiration, no joy, no creativity in this. But was this situation the result of some personal inadequacy on our part? Was there some fatal flaw built into Dan's and my psyche destined to self-destruct just at the moment of our apparent triumph?

What about those hard-edged executives we read about daily on the business pages, glibly swimming with the sharks, relentlessly searching for excellence, taking their guerilla marketing battles to the streets of the marketplace? In those days, before the fall of Trump, Milken and Helmsley, the role models for ambition and success glared at us endlessly from the glossy pages of advertisements and national business magazines.

And then there were the movie moguls—the stars, the directors, the producers—who crowed about their latest films, their charity benefits, their fitness routines, not to mention their highly publicized deep and rich relationships with their impeccably dressed, precious children. Were we not equally worthy of the American dream?

I mentally switched channels, shining the flickering electronic light on each of my friends and associates who likewise seemed to have it all. Our peers did precious little romping. In fact, at that moment, I couldn't think of a single individual in my fast-track pack of successful, upwardly mobile professionals who didn't look just as beaten as I felt. We were not fulfilling our potential—we were exhausting it.

Those of us savvy enough to realize we were burning out also expected that if only we meditated, exercised and ate nutritiously, our emotions would be handled. We didn't just feel bad. We felt bad about feeling bad.

I took a leap. Perhaps, I surmised, the fact that having it all took so much out of us was not proof of some inadequacy on our part. Rather, it was the symptom of the unhealthy expectations and closely guarded societal illusions that had infected an entire generation.

I vowed to do whatever it would take to reclaim time and space in our life. I would recruit Dan to help me explore and re-define ambition and success for our careers and business. Nothing would be sacred. Not the car phone. Not the Porsche. Not even the house.

Dan wasn't thrilled. Sell the house? We'd just bought the house. But I persisted. After some time, he nobly volunteered to continue with all of his responsibilities at the office, adding a chunk of mine as well, so that I could regain balance in my life. During the ensuing six months, I got happier and healthier working forty-hour weeks—what to our generation was considered part-time work. Dan, on the other hand, began developing various stress-related ailments, in increasingly serious progression.

After several more months of fervent debate, Dan finally agreed to join the revolution in earnest. We reduced the size of our business, cutting our hours back to between thirty and forty or so a week each. We were willing to pay for our newfound freedom by living in reduced circumstances.

We put our dream home up for sale and made plans to move to a more modest cottage.

Extolling the virtues of downward mobility, we went public with our story. Values before profit became our rallying cry, as we shared our message with Jane Pauley on *The Today Show* and Erma Bombeck on *Good Morning America*, among many others. "It is worth the sacrifice to reclaim time and space in your life," we proclaimed.

So why, on that balmy spring day not that long ago, did I find myself facing an audience of my peers, sweating out a living nightmare worse than my childhood fears?

Because just before going on stage, I had checked in with Dan, holding down the fort at our San Francisco office. The first quarter earnings for our company had just been phoned in by our accountant. They were up.

And this wasn't the first time.

The truth is that for nearly one full year, the trend toward downward mobility had been in reverse. Our dramatically smaller staff was handling virtually the same load of accounts we had held at the height of our super-business days. And we were doing this working at a comfortable pace. Our profits were exceeding industry averages month after month.

Here I was telling the finest businesspeople in the South that there were more important things than making money while our bank account was reaching all-time highs. This wasn't just a matter of forgetting my steps. This, I realized mid-speech, was a matter requiring entirely new choreography. The evidence was incontestable, but hardly believable. We had sliced our hours; suggested to our staff that they cut out overtime; let go of our impressive trappings – and were now more successful than ever. As I pondered this new information, I left a heavily weighted pause. To the sound of spoons hitting the sidewalls of ice cream dishes, I formulated the thesis that comprises the heart and soul of this book:

> Personal values and quality of life considerations need not conflict with ambition and success. In fact, it is from these very qualities that success will grow.

When I resumed talking, I put away my well-worn notes and began pouring out my revelations-in-process. The audience had been fully prepared to swallow the concept of downward mobility as the bitter pill of financial punishment for the spiritual rewards of incorporating personal values into their lives.

But the contentions that I am putting forth in this book, as they emerged that day in the form of a stream-of-consciousness confessional, sounded like the ravings of a madwoman. There was polite applause at the end of the lunch. But one response on my comment cards said it all: "Get Real."

By the time I arrived home, I knew I was in for some serious reassessment. How could I continue to sell people on downward mobility while Dan and I busied ourselves putting our profits into a growing portfolio of real estate investments? How could I tell my audiences to get off the fast track while I, myself, was jetting from city to city doing speeches and media appearances?

There was no discrepancy. I knew this in my gut. But who would believe me? Even I could not yet explain why things were turning out this way. I needed to take a break from the public spotlight to give my fledgling theories time to mature.

On long walks, in meditation, and in my journal, I asked myself the tough questions. Was this some kind of a fluke? Would this work for other people? Dan and I continued to run the business, testing our new ways of approaching our responsibilities through year after year of balance sheets. We practiced the principles shared in this book, seeing that they worked through crisis as well as triumph. Meanwhile, I attempted to put the concepts that were working so well for us into words, giving voice to what was turning out to be no less than a new work ethic, emerging from our generation of leadership.

Over time, using our own careers and business as the guinea

pig, we formulated our philosophy into seven radical principles. Unlike other success advice on the business bookshelf today, the principles that I share in this book are not simply techniques and strategies. These do not teach how to manipulate others for the purpose of obtaining power, the "old paradigm" that Stephen R. Covey unmasks so convincingly in his book *The Seven Habits of Highly Effective People* (Simon and Schuster, 1989). Rather, they are an entry into the deeper philosophical perspectives that consciously or unconsciously shape our relationship to ambition and success.

They provide the foundation of understanding that must be acknowledged before any of the more superficial business management strategies and advice available in the marketplace today can function for other than temporary gain.

As Overachievers Anonymous has continued, networking with businesspeople across the country through newsletter, speeches and conversation, we have had the opportunity to see these principles tested on many companies and individuals in the workplace, in addition to our own. From accountants to middle managers in manufacturing companies, from artists to contractors, from salespeople to retailers and restaurateurs: the principles in this book apply.

The conclusion many of us have been astonished by is what I will share with you in this book.

You can work less and achieve more. In fact, these radical precepts will transform your ambition and your process (the ability to respond, incorporate and act upon information from within and without), as well as your results into an experience of success that exceeds your wildest dreams. You may find a thousand reasons why, while these precepts may have worked for us, they won't work for you. They can work for you anyway. Prepare to be surprised.

PART I
THE CHALLENGE

LIFE-DRIVEN BUSINESS

*The competitive edge in the coming decades will
be held by those individuals and companies who
can tap into new, life-driven sources of
inspiration, creativity and vitality.*

OVERACHIEVERS ANONYMOUS was founded on the premise
that there has to be something more in life than success
born at the expense of your personal and spiritual needs
and values. The premise of this book is that the "something more" I found can lead you to an even greater experience of
success.

Both premises come from the same root: the recognition that
traditional approaches to "making it" were no longer working for
myself, nor for the majority of people of my generation.

Before exploring the reasons for this, let us consider what
these traditional approaches entailed. One of The Orsborn
Group's clients, the owner of a chain of restaurants, invited me to
hear his keynote address at their annual management meeting.

The story he shared—one which, I've since been told, is a motivational classic—will put us in the general philosophical barnyard:

Once upon a time, a chicken and a pig bumped into each other.

"I'm more important than you are," bragged the pig.

"Oh no you're not," replied the chicken. "Whenever the master wants breakfast, he always calls on me."

The pig sneered.

"That's just the point. When it comes to breakfast, the difference between you and me is that you participate—but I'm committed."

The owner of the chain concluded this inspirational story by adding that we should all be like the pig, fully committed.

After the session, he asked me what I thought of his presentation.

"The point of the story is that you want us to be committed—like the pig?" I mustered up my courage as best I could. After all, this was a client who represented a fair amount of revenue to our firm. "But Stan," I lowered my voice to a whisper, "the pig dies."

Stan is a reasonable man. He is a good father to his children—when he sees them for a couple of hours every other weekend or so. He respects his wife—when he can catch glimpses of her between her charity fundraisers, dedicated to assisting the restaurant chain in keeping its high community profile. He even cares about his employees—when they bring in the numbers he sets for them.

But Stan is caught up in a web of business practices and philosophies, spoken and unspoken, that cause him to hold up self-destructive ideals for himself and his employees on a daily basis.

When Stan grew up, in the heart of the fifties and early sixties, the Horatio Alger myth had some real juice in it. The presumption was that hard work would be rewarded with success. It is a simple formula, holding great sway with those of us who grew up in its shadow. If only it had proven to be true.

Facing increased competition from too many people fighting for too many slots—first in the finer colleges, then for jobs, now for promotions in the truncated corporate pyramids that have stalled more than one fine career—our generation has made the forty-hour work week, for which most of us are paid, an anachronism. The fifty- and sixty-hour work weeks, which in the day of the gray flannel suit was a sign of the divinely inspired—or at least the divinely driven—have in the nineties, become the norm. Now, to work harder and longer, one must differentiate one's self from the masses by working around the clock. Our clients in the hotel business have always understood this concept. For them, the client literally moves in. There are virtually no vacations and no weekends. In fact, one of the primary perks offered top hotel management is housing on the premises.

For the rest of us, living in the age of the global economy, when at any given time somebody is getting up and getting dressed for work as somewhere in the world a stock market is opening, the twenty-four–hour day has become a literal reality.

A trip to the newsstand can reveal a frightening portrait of contemporary success. In glossy advertisements in our major business and news magazines, executives can find their favorite clothing shop still open at 8 P.M. ready to press their clothes for their next round of meetings. Then it's to the airport, arriving at the hotel at midnight to be greeted by an urgent fax. The deal is concluded by long-distance phone, overseas, at 3 A.M. We are on the fast track to success, briefcases flying, gasping for air. These images are not the personification of inspiration. Scratch the surface of the quest for excellence, and you will find images that are anxious and fearful. At some point in the past several years, the anxiety-motivated pace of American business surpassed the limits of human endurance. The old strategies for success—trying harder and working smarter, providing service or product above and beyond what the competition is also willing and able to deliver—have, quite simply, broken down.

In the case of Stan's chain of restaurants, the implications of his inspirational story were immediate and terrible. After listening to the story of the Chicken and the Pig, the managers of the restaurants in the chain left the smoke-filled room to fight the good fight. Whenever I stopped by, morning, night, weekends, I saw them giving their all. On deeper inspection, I learned that a number of them were fueling their all with uppers and cocaine.

By the time the next marketing meeting rolled around, one of the managers had proven to be just as committed as the pig. While on the job, he suffered a fatal heart attack, leaving behind a wife and several young children.

Living up to our society's role models for success, we give everything we've got—and more. Isn't it ironic, then, that despite our extraordinary commitment to our careers and businesses, so many of our major industries and financial institutions are in shambles? What have we accomplished with all this commitment? We have done little more than create a workforce that is unhealthy and dispirited. Deprived by our anxiety-driven pace of the subtler human qualities that would otherwise provide perspective and meaning, we find ourselves in an emotional vacuum. Driven by fear, we grab what little we can for ourselves, establishing the destructive reciprocities that eventually result in a society dominated by greed and self-interest.

At the manager's funeral, everybody blamed increasing competition in the marketplace for the pressure he and they were under. The experts tell us that the pressure from outside ourselves to keep up the pace will only increase over the coming years. As *Fortune* ("Is Your Company Asking Too Much?" March 12, 1990) warns: "America's top corporate chiefs think your work week looks like a picnic compared to what's ahead in the age of global competition." And yet, the greatest stress on that organization had nothing to do with anything that came from the outside. It had to do with massive turnover caused by burnout, dismissal for drug use, and now death. It had to do with poor interpersonal relationships between managers and staff, fueled by resentment and guilt. And it had to do with the impact of fear and stress on the individual manager's ability to think clearly and creatively.

In a recent survey of the readership of "Inner Excellence: The Bulletin of Business and Spirituality," I asked the question "Do you think at some point, working harder and longer can become counterproductive?"

I had several hundred responses to my survey, coming from twenty industries in twelve states. My correspondents included a partner in a CPA firm; the executive vice president of a fundraising group; middle managers in manufacturing, utility companies, aerospace and high-tech companies; technical professionals, such as mechanical engineers and lab technicians; health professionals, including doctors, psychologists and nurses. There were photographers, secretaries, presidents of advertising agencies and personnel firms; management consultants and real estate salespeople, among others.

The response was unanimous:

"Working harder and longer can lead to desperation, which leads to panic and then loss of confidence and self-control. Who could succeed feeling those feelings?"

"A slower, more realistic way of scheduling work is more productive in the long run. There are fewer mistakes, fewer false starts, better concentration, higher morale and greater creativity. This shows up directly in the quality of results."

"We have got to have uninterrupted time to think and create.

You can't get this if you are working for somebody who is willing to sacrifice their own sanity—as well as yours—for the sake of short-term results. It is the job of people in management to model a healthy life with time for work, relationships, recreation, creativity and so on. Then work can take on an appropriate role in our lives."

Just as we give hurricanes names like "Hugo," the Japanese have given death from overwork a name. They call it *karoshi*. But they are not the same. Globalization and increased competition, however awesome they seem to those of us perched on the brink, are not natural phenomena.

We forget that every reason offered to justify the pressure on us to explore the outer reaches of human endurance derives from phenomena that are strictly, unequivocally man-made. If we are to be something other than victims of worldwide *karoshi*, we must take a deeper look at the source of this new breed of "natural" disaster. This is no small matter. To do so, we must adopt new ways of thinking that run counter to virtually every precept of traditional American business philosophy. Taking the leap to implementing the principles in this book may be, in fact, a desperate act. In this regard, then—providing the impetus for taking the risk—desperation may actually serve a useful purpose.

It was out of desperation, for instance, that Dan and I gave up turning to traditional business management and inspiration books for advice. What good was it to have our top business experts tell us that the way to gain the edge was to work harder and longer than our competitors if our competitors were reading the same books? We ransacked the shelves of our local bookstores, bypassing the business books and turning to alternate sources for inspiration.

I was astonished to discover that it was saints, heroes and mystics from times long past whose insights and parables offered the most concrete and immediately applicable guidance. From myth to literature, from folklore to history: I began the task of translating esoteric images into the language of contemporary business success.

Although I brandished the briefcase of the executive rather than the sword of the hero, I came to realize that I was just as surely on a heroic quest. The prize I sought may have been career satisfaction and profitability, rather than the Golden Fleece, but I soon began to understand that the hero's internal process was the same long ago as it is for me in today's marketplace. The challenges I face in my career and business—and, it became increasingly apparent to me, faced by the American workplace in general—are now, as it was for the heroes back then, essentially spiritual in nature.

The word spirituality connotes many things to many people, so I will define it cautiously. I am not speaking of valentine hearts and cupids circling in a childlike homage to love and peace. Nor am I addressing what many experience as the constricting trappings of religion.

In this book, spirituality refers to that deeply alive place within each of us that longs for fulfillment. This inner longing, when acknowledged, can be a task master far more demanding than the external prods to action that many of us currently allow to call the shots in our busy lives. Envisioned as a wall of fire or a fierce dragon, heroic spirituality calls us forth to meet life on life's terms.

You must find qualities within yourself you did not know you possessed.

You must be willing to venture beyond your own comfort zone to journey where no one has ever gone before: into the recesses of your own heart.

I am not talking about leaving the world of ambition and success to find peace by escaping to a less demanding life. I am talking about being willing to venture inward to find new sources of inspiration for practical application to your life. When it is internally generated inspiration that motivates your worklife—replacing externally reactive fear as the impetus to perform—you have a career and business that is driven by life rather than fear. In this book, I refer to this new paradigm as "life-driven."

Courage to make the shift from a fear-driven to life-driven paradigm is required because of our society's bias against looking within for alternatives.

Psychologist Abraham Maslow once explained that in western culture, we have been taught not to trust ourselves—not to trust that we do know what we most deeply desire, and how to resolve our inner conflicts. We have been taught that beneath the veneer of the socialized conscious mind lurk who-knows-what animal urges, repressed hostilities and other evils. We have been taught not to risk exploring the unconscious mind.

When Dan and I reduced the size of The Orsborn Group, many of the staff left willingly. They understood that if they stayed they would have to play in an entirely new ballgame. As much as we may kick and complain about our disappointing lives and jobs, it is preferable for many of us to spend our days combatting bosses and clients who demand too much, the rotten economy, bills and debts and taxes, than to take the leap within.

Three thousand years ago, the *I Ching*, the Chinese book of philosophy, explained to its more serious students that once an individual has faced the fear of looking honestly into his own heart, he will never fear any threat that comes from outside himself again.

This advice holds the key to power, with direct practical application to your career, business and life; but the door it unlocks is to a humility that seems the very antithesis of our contemporary understanding of ambition and success.

Is it worth the risk to open this door? If you truly want to have the experience of success, what is your alternative? You are already bright enough, educated enough; you have already worked hard enough and smart enough; you have already striven for excellence enough. You have done enough of what is no longer working for you. Do you want to find the competitive edge that will work for you now? Then you're going to have to try something new.

RECLAIMING OUR HUMAN RESOURCES

*The unrest you are experiencing is not
individual psychological difficulty but rather,
part of a widespread spiritual awakening.*

Aﬀer THE restaurant manager's funeral, Stan called his staff
and consultants together to give us a pep talk.

"With Kevin gone, we are going to have to pull together
and work even harder to reach our goals."

Not long thereafter, the chain received a second blow. One of
the country's prominent restaurant review guidebooks down-
graded their rating, taking away one of their coveted stars.

After a profitable ten-year relationship, I resigned representation of Stan's restaurant chain. Still Stan did not get the message.
Those who persist in driving their careers and businesses while
looking solely in the rearview mirror, are sooner or later going to
have an accident. The Big Eight accounting firms; the airlines; the
entire savings and loan industry: the turn of the decade looked
more like an army surplus warehouse for obsolete and wrecked

vehicles than the noble economic battlefield in which we had been geared for combat.

The fact that you are reading these principles today is not coincidence. We are all being influenced by our generation: the massive number of post-World War II boom babies hitting midlife just as we are moving into positions of power in virtually every industry. As this influential group hits midlife, we find ourselves engulfed by careers at an age when we are increasingly questioning the philosophical foundations of our lives. Having attained positions of authority in virtually every career sector, we are bridling beneath the anxiety-fueled motivations that we passively adopted over the past two decades. Response to Overachievers Anonymous is evidence of this. An increasing number of us now believe that the growing unrest we are experiencing is not individual psychological difficulty but rather, a healthy spiritual awakening.

The generation coming into power has had unprecedented mobility, access to expanded resources and information – and the education to appreciate and use them. Many of us are using this information drawn from other times and places as a springboard for our emerging beliefs. What in many other societies would have constituted "secret knowledge," garbed in esoteric language and obtuse imagery available only to an elite, is available for all of us to incorporate into our everyday lives.

The thousands of successful individuals from across the country who are responding to the call for a new work ethic are harbingers of a new era for business, an age when personal values, spirit, and integrity are not checked at the door as we hit our offices. We are demonstrating every day that the approach embodied in this book has practical, profitable implications.

With this spirit to spark the fuse, the American business mainstream is destined to experience no less than a revolution in the way we approach our careers and companies. In life-driven careers and businesses, people work at a pace that enhances their vitality, allowing them the time to refuel themselves with self-nurturing. Employers and employees keep the lines of communication open and honest, understanding that overall, the needs of the individual are consistent with what is best for the business. This cannot be accomplished in an environment motivated primarily by fear. Anxiety and stress over time decrease our ability to perform. Only in a life-driven environment can we hope to fulfill our potential not only as workers–but as human beings.

In my recent survey of members, I also asked the question "Can you think of ways your company/affiliation has been able to reduce anxiety in the workplace?"

Companies across the country have instituted mental health days in addition to vacation or sick time where employees can choose to spend time away from the office to revitalize.

"In our office," one of my correspondents wrote, "when someone reports that they are home with the flu, I am pretty certain that I won't stumble across them at the baseball game, or out shopping with their children. This is simply because we encourage our employees to take the time and space for themselves in their work day and schedules to live a balanced life."

One company offers stress management workshops teaching employees how to apply the principles of aikido in the corporate environment; another has set aside a space in the office for meditation. The office of a county assessor and treasurer has initiated a quiet-time policy for the eighty-person office. Six of the workers screen phone calls and handle customers from 8:30 to 10:30 A.M. every day. Doors are closed and meetings are postponed. Everyone, with the exception of the six on call, has uninterrupted time. Five months after starting this program, staff reported that the backlog of work was reduced considerably.

Many correspondents reported replacing the power lunch and its time-consuming quasi-social ambiance, with a quiet solo stroll through the corporate environs, utilizing the precious moments midday to relax and revitalize rather than perform or entertain. Life-driven workers trust that they will have the time and energy to build a fulfilling life outside of normal work hours. As a result, the time spent in meetings and social functions that previously gave the overachiever the false impression that he or she had a satisfying social life can instead be invested in activities more to the point of business.

At The Orsborn Group, people are encouraged to leave the office by 5:30 and to use their full vacation time. When they are sitting at their desks looking overwhelmed by the stacks of work, they are not prodded to work faster, harder or longer. Top management acts on the theory that if the company is staffed adequately, employees will find the solution to handling the backup within the normal work day more readilly through support and trust than through fear and desperation.

The Orsborn Group creates a culture that honors outside hobbies and interests, bending as it can to accommodate requests for flex-time; job-sharing and other creative options. Ironically, it is not unusual for the agency's employees to admit, with some astonishment, that working in such a life-driven environment actually inspires them to exceed previous levels of commitment and effort. The key is to choose each moment of every day what is the appropriate and most productive level of energy to invest in one's work at any given time. Each member of the agency team has the capacity and willingness to rise to the occasion, whatever that occasion might be.

There are periods when producing at the outer reaches of endurance and ability for an extended period of time is necessary and even nurturing. I do not, for instance, regret the long hours I invested in the early years of building our business. Dan has recently taken the lead in establishing a professional services section for our region's chapter of the Public Relations Society of America, simultaneously having been elected to serve as chairman of the national section. I have no problem burning the midnight oil while driven by inspiration to capture some exciting new thought for this book.

At the same time, working in a highly competitive industry, it would be dishonest to give the impression that we never feel the pressure of impossible deadlines and clients' demands. At those times if it isn't fear that packs home paperwork to tackle after the kids are tucked in for the night, it does a pretty good imitation.

The real problem comes, however, when I—or any of us—go into unconscious overdrive, forgetting to shift back out of high gear after such a bout with adrenaline has served its purpose.

From the outside, the life-driven business or career may look no different than one that is fueled by fear. Sightseers hoping to catch the Orsborn Group staff taking an afternoon nap are likely to be disappointed.

People are at their desks, busy at work. Phones are ringing. Packages are delivered, deadlines set and kept.

Recently I received a phone call from a job applicant, scheduled to have arrived for her interview with me twenty minutes earlier.

"I'm behind on my schedule today," she reported cheerily. "I started to panic, until I realized who it was I was going to be meeting. I was certain you would understand if I chose not to make myself crazy rushing and came to see you an hour late."

"I understand," I replied. "But I won't be here."

Life-driven business is not about lowering standards or results. It is, rather, about the reclamation of vitality, creativity and natural inspiration from that most important of business assets: our human resources. In the life-driven business, the habit of hard work driven by fear is replaced by a dedication to service and results.

Inc. magazine (July, 1989) published the story of a factory owner in Massachusetts whose sales had picked up significantly. He noticed that his workers were responding to the pressure to produce by pushing their hours to the point that ten-hour days became the norm.

The owner crunched some numbers, confirming his suspicions: no more was being produced in the ten-hour days than had been produced in the bygone era of eight-hour days before business picked up. There were more accidents and morale was down.

The owner ended overtime for factory and office workers and scheduled a second shift. By revitalizing his workforce, he got a more efficient factory floor. Accidents declined. Soon he was able to compensate his workers for the lost overtime by issuing three extra paychecks a year, made possible by higher productivity.

In such an environment, bosses and employees are much more apt to be creative, to take reasonable risks and to derive personal satisfaction from work.

Companies who believe in these principles are still relatively few in number, but the number is growing rapidly. As CEOs come to realize that there is a positive correlation between these principles and the bottom line, we will see the life-driven business philosophy become the number one perk of the coming decades.

Just as in the 1980s, when high-tech and financial companies competed for employees by appealing to greed, companies are now discovering that the way to win the top candidates is with promises of forty-hour or less work weeks, flexible schedules, on-premise childcare and extracurricular activities, like company choirs and reading clubs.

Levi Strauss, Inc., under the leadership of Robert D. Haas, has already taken strides in establishing a culture that supports their employees' right to a balanced life.

In the Levi Strauss Aspirations Statement, employees are told,

> We want our people to feel respected, treated fairly, listened to and involved. Above all, we want satisfaction from accomplishments and friendships, balanced personal and professional lives, and to have fun in our endeavors.
>
> What type of leadership is necessary to make our aspirations a reality? New behaviors. Leadership that exemplifies directness, openness to influence, commitment to the success of others, willingness to acknowledge our own contributions to problems, personal accountability, teamwork and trust. Not only must we model these behaviors but we must coach others to adopt them.

Robert Haas responded to early word of Overachievers Anonymous by commenting, "I heartily endorse your concept of encouraging people to reexamine their priorities and achieve a balance between their business and personal lives."

The philosophy has paid off for Levi Strauss in the continually increasing pool of eager, qualified applicants vying to work for the firm. Soaring profits regularly make headline news.

But we can't all work for Levi Strauss, or maybe not even any of the 5000 individuals and companies who have supported the concepts of Overachievers Anonymous. How about the rest of us?

There is an answer. The Seven Principles of Life-Driven Business that comprise the heart of this book will point the way.

PART II

THE SEVEN PRINCIPLES
OF LIFE-DRIVEN BUSINESS

PRINCIPLE NUMBER ONE

*Change your beliefs about the nature of business
and of life, and you will change how you
manage your career.*

W**HILE WE** are waiting for the American business climate to catch up with our philosophical ideals, the vast majority of us have bosses who are too demanding, clients who are too unappreciative. We need the income. Our families depend on us. We have responsibilities.

And underneath all of this, holding it up and keeping it going, we also have our deeply held beliefs.

The beliefs you hold about the nature of business and of life determine how you will manage your career. Joseph Campbell, conversing with Bill Moyers as recorded in their book *The Power of Myth* (Doubleday, 1988), described the relationship between our beliefs and our subsequent manifestations as a computer program. You enter the data, and the computer will respond according to your commands. Campbell admitted that "he likes to play with the software," adding new ideas as they cross his path. Moyers suggested that some of the greatest saints borrowed from anywhere they could.

"They have taken from this and from that, and constructed a new software."

To reprogram your belief system, you must prepare yourself to hang in for the long run. You must be willing to stay with it long enough to gather the tools and resources, load the program and work out the bugs. You will have to work at it over time.

The fact that developing a new set of beliefs takes work runs counter to the slick and easy faith we encounter in our media-fueled world of junk food theology: just enough wisdom to sate our appetite, but not enough to offer long-term nourishment. We like our spirituality packaged for us by Shirley MacLaine, with enough snappy stories to make her a good talk show guest and sufficient theatrics to land her a television movie of the week. We choke up when our sports heroes and Oscar winners give the credit for their personal triumphs to God—but cut away to commercials when things go wrong.

Our consciousness trainers have epiphanies while driving down the superhighways of life at 65 miles per hour. We can get "it," whatever "it" turns out to be, in a weekend workshop. Gurus offer spontaneous enlightenment at the tap of a peacock feather. We are set up for dramatic, instantaneous transformation—unprepared for the reality of the commitment it takes to lay groundwork for the integration of spirit and success.

The irony is that in spiritual belief systems, you are asked to exert the greatest investment of energy, discipline and commitment when you have the least evidence that it will be worth it. As anyone who has struggled with his or her resistance to computers knows, as long as the desire for comfort takes precedence over the willingness to defer gratification, results will be handicapped by the old technology. In spiritual belief systems, as in software, you progress only when you are willing to take a leap of faith.

Bringing your internal "programming" to awareness is not an easy task. It is the very pervasiveness of your assumptions that blind you to them. If you hold your world view unconsciously, you will be the victim of your beliefs. You will have no choice about critical factors that determine your actions and responses on a day-to-day basis. The alternative is to bring them to consciousness through honesty and self-evaluation. Only then will you have a say about the assumptions and beliefs that you ultimately choose to adopt, and that will color your decisions and behavior on the job and in your life.

Several nights ago, Dan and I were invited to a blues bash, given by a prominent local lawyer for his clients and friends. Chatting our way around the room, we were able to catch snippets of conversation.

A seasoned executive shared his wisdom with a young associate, who leaned eagerly toward his mentor at the bar.

"If you are going to succeed, you've got to put the demands of your job first."

"Susan is serious about her career," the female half of a couple commented between sips. "She's always working."

Above the cool jazz tones, two men in pinstripes bragged about the fierce marketing battle their firm had waged against a competitor.

"Business is like war," one exclaimed.

"It's us or it's them," the second agreed.

Taking some well-earned "r and r" in this cozy environment of blues and booze, many of these businesspeople—had they been challenged—would have defined themselves as "realists." As realists, we adopt and act on assumptions that are universally accepted as true.

Unfortunately, in our society—as reflected in the statements overheard at our associate's soirée—the primary impetus for our ambition is externally motivated.

"He who works hardest, longest and toughest, wins."

Is business a fearsome battlefield, and your clients, your employees, your bosses and peers—not to mention your family and friends—the inevitable casualties? You fight for market share, "beat the competition" at all costs . . . and hold beliefs that allow you to make self-destructive decisions over and over again.

A customer makes a harsh remark and you are thrust into over-drive, calling upon your knowledge and responses to put yourself back on top. You are passed over for a promotion. You've got to prove yourself.

A young driver was sent to guide me through a maze of media

interviews in Seattle. On a tight schedule, she panicked at the first stoplight over whether she could get us to our next appointment on time. Our car careened into the front drive of a television station parking lot, with a few precious moments to spare.

"Follow me!" she shouted, jumping out and disappearing around the corner of the production facility. We were in a dead run.

"Around here!" she rounded corner number two. "It's just a little farther."

As she disappeared once again, I heard her voice dimly in the distance: "It's the next one" wafted back to me from around corner three.

We were back exactly where we had begun: at the front entrance to the station.

We both survived this tangle with desperation. But not everyone is this lucky. One anecdote making the rounds of advertising agencies is that of a New York art director, responsible for delivering top quality work for what is considered to be one of the most demanding yet capricious clients in the business. Keeping the client meant not just assuring the ongoing viability of the agency as a whole, but keeping his job.

On this particular day, he was hailing a cab, rushing to meet a routine deadline, when he suffered a stroke. As he fell, he maneuvered himself in such a way that he landed on the wet snow and managed to keep his client's paste-up boards dry.

A hand-scrawled poster on one of my client's bulletin boards summarizes my feelings about the kind of desperation we see in the workplace on a routine basis:

"We don't need any desperation, thank you. We are already oversupplied."

If it is true that you are getting sick and tired of being chased through your career with fear biting at your heels, why are you so willing to accept anxiety-induced motivation as the primary fuel for your ambition? Why do you engage in the self-destructive reciprocities that create a climate that is unhealthy for us all?

We can begin to get a handle on this by observing how many of our business environment's commonly accepted beliefs come disguised in seductive packaging, not unlike the sirens luring Odysseus' crew to death with their irresistible voices. In the contemporary success mythology, the sirens call out to us again—and the songs they sing are "work hard and you will be rewarded," and "you deserve to have it all."

From the time you are old enough to understand that the jolly old man with the fat tummy only brings presents to good little girls and boys, you get the picture about reward and punishment. You are processed through grammar school grading systems, textbook fables and childhood heroes, and well-meaning parents exacting disciplined behavior from you in exchange for love. Even heaven awaits those of you who get the message.

You grow up to believe that if you could only be good enough, work hard enough, get it right enough you can get your career and your business to turn out just the way you want them to. Tell enough people that if they try hard enough they can control their outcomes, and what do you get? A society of superachievers, running as fast as we can but getting nowhere because we are struggling to hold back the possibility that anything not to our custom-ordered specifications will happen.

The closer you are to achieving your goals, the more likely you are to be engaged in this struggle. You have done so much, you are so close to "having it all," that you actually believe that giving that extra ounce of energy and effort might close the gap. In fact, this was the bait that led me into the mega work week: not being hopelessly far behind; but rather, being so tantalizingly close.

This impulse to perform is further advanced by modern science. As Willis Harman, Ph.D. points out in his book *Global Mind Change* (Knowledge Systems, Inc., 1988) the past century has made it possible for us to exert an unprecedented influence on nature, fending off the dark with electric lights, taming bacteria with antibiotics. It is this—the ability to apply external solutions to what, in previous centuries, would have forced us to come to terms with awesome forces of the universe—that has supported our operative belief systems.

In the scientific era, so many of the "miracles" we once thought to be beyond rational understanding have been replicated on demand. Microscopic cameras probe the inner struggles of the sperm as it navigates upstream to star on prime-time educational television programs. Skeletons are uncovered from the earth's deep stratas, filling in the gaps concerning our species' history.

Many of us have found ourselves faced with the choice of choosing between scientific information and our spiritual beliefs.

The very act of accepting the miraculous – devoid of the need, or even the possibility of logical explanation – forced our ancestors to surrender a piece of their rational minds, making both the room and the necessity for faith. For all the plagues and pestilence, each individual knew that his or her only hope for inner peace was to call some kind of truce with the universe.

We, on the other hand, have seen no compelling reason to cultivate faith. Anything we didn't learn in science classes will find its way sooner or later onto the evening news. Want to get pregnant? Don't want to die? The best minds in the world are at work solving whatever riddles yet remain.

We, whose inheritance has been the western rational mind, live in a world of expanded choices. We have religious freedom, the democratic system of government, upward and downward mobility, liberation of race and of gender. The only freedom we have relinquished is our ability to surrender to the irrational. Like young children, we put our superhero capes over our pinstriped suits, stamp our feet, and proclaim to the universe, "I can do it by myself."

To help make sense of the meaning of life, consumerism has stepped in where faith once served. We are not forced to learn humility before an unpredictable universe. We simply add more "things" to our lives, each thing designed to postpone discomfort.

We believe that there is no problem or pain so serious that it can't be temporarily relieved by a new job, a new employee, a new piece of equipment, a raise. Our economy also depends on us to add more "things" to our lives. We try everything we can think of to avoid and limit disappointment.

Many of us have been discovering that in the race to the finish line, we have large gaps in our understanding about life. We have learned how to make some money—or, at the very least, how to use lines of credit. We have learned how to start and raise families. Some of us have even taken great strides towards making contributions to society through work and social involvements. But we have not yet begun to understand what it takes to be at peace.

Why? The program is flawed.

The programming we have accepted teaches us that we can judge ourselves and others on the basis of our ability to avoid discomfort and disappointment. We invest our energy trying to control our reality—altering the circumstances with which we are faced. But if we believe we are rewarded for how good we are, then when things go wrong—as, sooner or later, they inevitably will—it must be our fault. We, who are so willing to be held accountable for our results and our creations, have only been prepared to win.

By mid-career, our efforts to perform and accumulate lure us into lifestyles built on the untrustworthy sands of reward and punishment. The more we throw onto our careers and businesses, the more complex and demanding the management problem we face. As fast as our salaries and companies grow, our expenses and overhead grow faster.

This happened to one of The Orsborn Group's consultants, a small law practice who decided that the way to success was to take big, glamorous space in the top building in the downtown financial district. To justify the space, they added staff. To pay for the overhead, they raised their fees. Within six months, the lawyers had alienated their client base by assigning new associates to the work while charging higher prices. In the end, they only got one major assignment: doing the paperwork on their own dissolution.

Before long, the drive for "more" transforms from straight-ahead ambition fueled by the drive for control, to the convoluted compulsion to shore up the breaches in the structure at all costs. When you reach this critical stage, you may truly believe that your best hope is to stay so busy you don't have the time to admit you have already bitten off more than you can chew.

No wonder you are afraid. You are scared that your competitors are getting the upper hand. Scared of demanding bosses, losing clients, losing business, losing ground. Scared of losing your spouse to another man or woman; your children to drugs; your health to stress.

Ironically, however, it is fear itself that is the richest breeding ground for inferior performance. Who is at their best when they are fearful? Where are creativity and vitality? Where is self-confidence, encouraging the taking of risks? Where is authenticity —the willingness to speak honestly and take the consequences? Fearful thinking damages you by encouraging you to cross the line between responsibility and blame. You judge yourself, those who report to you and the world around you harshly. You fear receiving from others what you are so ready and willing to dish out.

"Like all people, managers behave according to their assumptions of how the world works—whether, for instance, it is a kind or a cruel place. Disastrous behavior follows when a manager's assumptions about the world establish a dangerous and self-defeating pattern," explains Professor Louis B. Barnes, D.B.A., of Harvard University Business School, an advisor to the Over-achievers Anonymous newsletter ("Managing the Paradox of Organizational Trust," *Harvard Business Review*, March 1981).

It has become commonplace to the point that it barely raises an eyebrow when employees use their time at an organization to build customer loyalty to themselves, rather than the company. The staff stars incubate their own business within the confines of the parent company, leaving at some point with a big piece of the parent company with them.

In the public relations industry, you can pretty much predict the future when one of these mavericks sends out his or her self-congratulatory press release announcing the formation of the new, competitive firm.

You know that within three years, there will be another press release making the rounds. This one will be from the maverick's top executives, announcing that they are splitting off with a big piece of business to form their own competitive company.

"Obeying a distorted golden rule, people do to others what they perceive is being done to them," explains Professor Barnes.

"Beginning with a pervasive sense of mistrust, they shift eventually into a set of destructive reciprocities and finally to even more divisive and self-oriented needs."

As a result, our organizations run along brittle, authoritarian lines with subsequent waste of energy as individuals within the organization battle each other for control. When you hold the power in such an environment of fear, owning your own company or being the boss to a subordinate, you automatically protect your position by putting your employees on the defensive. Everyone is considered guilty until proven innocent.

Faced with accusatory tones, the employee has to wade through feelings of personal inadequacy, mounting an internal defense, before he or she can respond to even the most basic questions.

"Where's the report you promised me?"

"Why haven't you delivered those results?"

When faced with negative expectations, staff spends a good percentage of retained time reacting to real or implied threats. They find themselves spending more time reporting on what they are doing—and less time getting work done. More time is spent in meetings trying to "share" responsibility and avoid taking blame. On an internal level, precious creative energy is wasted processing the emotions of turmoil, often finding release through expressions of resentment.

When any individual is forced to operate out of this level of fear, he or she shuts out perspective and insight. Squelching intuition, he is forced to do everything the hard way. Devoid of inspiration, he resorts to faking excellence. When an anxious client or boss is breathing down his neck, a fearful employee is more likely to put on a show of hard work. He will call every prospect on his long lists to hit one who will say yes. The tone of desperation and resentment makes even that one a tough sell. In a more relaxed environment, he would be more likely to call upon his intuitive ability to make the one inspired call that would have garnered the same—or, more likely—superior results, leaving his potential capacity whole and healthy, rather than reactive and depleted.

Operating out of fear of bosses or clients is exhausting enough. But the real battle—the struggle that sets the stage for the enactment of the external drama—is internal. Sooner or later, each one of us must confront the real competition. In your struggle with yourself, you may be driven by the hope that your frantic efforts to manage your livelihood will be sufficient to eliminate pain. But you are just as likely to be glimpsing a different reality: the disillusionment that comes when you realize that your effort is doomed.

Which reality will win out? In our society, disillusionment is the more terrifying prospect because when you surrender the childlike belief that you can control the world by being good enough, there is nothing waiting in the wings to take its place. How are we to make peace with the universe?

In our consumer-driven society, many of the spiritual institutions we have turned to have become packagers of the kind of experiences we think we want, rather than challenge us to painful but potentially more fruitful possibilities. Meditations in some religious institutions are cut to five minutes or less—and even these truncated moments of contemplation are given a backdrop of easy-listening organ and choir, complete with soprano who sings aloud for us what our hearts are supposed to be feeling. Some religious institutions go so far as to market themselves on the basis of their superior sports facilities, their catering, their business network.

In consciousness, spirit and religion, you may be forced to suffer the superficial on one hand. But on the other, when you do find individuals or groups that have the potential to awaken the untapped powers you hold within your heart, you may expose your vulnerability only to find that you have opened yourself to the unscrupulous, the fraudulent, the power-hungry.

Many of these awakeners have crossed the line between empowering others and exploiting them. You are on dangerous turf when you are asked to go out and recruit new followers as evidence, loyalty or practice of your expanding mastery of spiritual beliefs or personal growth.

Even if the biggest risk you take is to read this book, you may have to grapple with an age-old challenge: how to get what you need by surrendering to something beyond your control, without losing yourself in the process. The only thing stronger than our desire to take a leap of faith to a life that has meaning, is the fear that we will be let down again.

You can continue to evade your disillusionment by running

even faster, chased through worlds of ambition by unspeakable fears—or you can, as this principle teaches, try something new.

What must you do to break the deadlock?

You, who pride yourself on your ability to do it by yourself, will not like the answer.

Accept irresolution.

Accept restlessness, insecurity and pain.

Let the great internal battles rage! Should you push ahead? Quit? What does it all mean? Is it hopeless?

There is a reality external to yourself over which you have no control. You cannot embark on the path that will lead you to the experience of true success until you confront the fact that work is tough and you can't always do something about it.

Is this depressing, or is this—as I contend in this book—liberating? It is not the fact that work is tough that stops you from experiencing success. Ironically, it is the degree to which fear of admitting this motivates your life that your businesses and careers will suffer. Unless you are willing to face the fact that you can never be good enough to fix everything that happens to you, the opportunity to live life fully will elude you. You will be too busy running away from ultimate truths, throwing your how-to books with their false promises of success into the bonfire of your deeper suspicions that you are destined to fail. If you suppress internal conflict, opting for busy, acquisitive responses to internal drives, you will be condemned to an ultimately unfulfilling existence.

It is your fundamental human right to have a trusting relationship with the universe that makes sense of your life. This longing for faith in the universe is legitimate. Just as you have physical needs for sufficient sleep and food, you have spiritual needs that you desire to have fulfilled. When you lose your connection to faith, you turn against yourself. You become angry at yourself for your restlessness—angry at your spiritual neediness. You try to blot out irresolution, punishing your yearning for a life that has meaning with what we have been taught to think of as greater and greater success.

If you suppress the yearning, you are doomed to be at the mercy of the pervasive beliefs that unconsciously shape every aspect of how you run your career.

The first step of the journey to life-driven business requires that you neither deny your pain nor try to control it by changing others, your situation or yourself. You must find it in your heart to sit patiently with complexity and imperfection without feeling compelled to find cursory resolution.

Many of you will not have the courage to go this route until you've exhausted every other possibility. However, only by surrendering your illusion of control can you hope to escape from the destructive urges that drive your ambition.

Principle Number One

Change your beliefs about the nature of business and of life, and you will change how you manage your career.

PRINCIPLE NUMBER TWO

In order to become fully successful,
you must first be fully alive.

W HEN YOU SURRENDER the illusion of control, there is only one way left to find fulfillment: by cultivating an appreciation for the full range of creativity and destruction that life contains. You cannot be fully successful unless you are fully alive.

When you surrender to life, you experience everything from ecstasy to despair. You submit to uncertainty and unconsciousness. The key is to give up resistance and accept where you are right now, no matter how uncomfortable that place may be.

There is no safety in this—no guarantees that you will get through unscratched. These life-driven principles require you to sacrifice the illusion of safety for the realization of what it means to be awake and alive.

The misguided attempt to protect yourself from pain may have come quietly, such as when you decide not to say to another what you really feel. When you keep busy in order to avoid your feelings. When you don't do what you know is right because you don't know why you should bother. When you show off to impress others. When you decide to do something good or nice simply to win the approval of others.

The temptation, always, is to give up your authenticity in the name of comfort; to preserve the status quo—however unsatisfying the status quo may be. Short-term, you make it look good. But over time, the weaknesses in the structure inevitably take their toll.

A friend of mine, Marsha, suffered the consequences of such a sacrifice. Managing the retail operations of a major international bank, Marsha had by her side a trusted protégé, Carl. Over the years, she shared more and more of her power with her associate. Eventually, despite her best intentions, she became dependent on him. Unfortunately, she did not realize this until the day he came to her, explaining that he had received a competitive job offer and was planning to leave.

Despite the fact that Marsha had managed the retail operations brilliantly for the several years prior to hiring Carl, she was willing to do whatever it took to keep him. Justifying her actions in the name of generosity, faith and gratitude, she dealt him most of her remaining power cards. She denied herself, her own competence and ability, to keep his loyalty.

While pledging his renewed allegiance to Marsha, Carl's outstanding work couldn't help but be recognized by Marsha's boss.

Eventually, when the opportunity presented itself, Carl was promoted over Marsha. Not long thereafter, Marsha left the bank.

By trying to protect herself, Marsha chose the very path that led her in the fastest and most direct way to the realization of her worst fears.

There is another way.

Here is my version of a story popular in Twelve Step circles.

An engineer was checking construction on the top floor of a partially completed highrise. He slipped on a beam, saving himself temporarily from a precipitous fall by grabbing on to it. Hanging forty floors above street level, the engineer felt the beam begin to slip.

This man had never believed in God, but felt that this was as good a time as any to begin.

"God, are you up there?"

"Yes, my son," God replied. "What can I do for you?"

"God, help me. Tell me what to do!" he cried.

"You really want to know?"

The beam slipped a bit more.

Desperate, he cried out again.

"Yes, God. Tell me!"

There was a moment's silence. Then God answered him.

"Let go of the beam."

"Let go of the beam?"

"Yes, my son. Let go of the beam."

There was another moment's silence, then the engineer spoke.

"Is there anybody else up there?"

You say you want success, the kind of success that will last? The price is steep. You have wasted so much precious time and energy operating under the pretense that you are in charge.

Admitting helplessness is a last, desperate resort. When you find the courage to let go of your illusions, you condemn yourself to the willingness to experience despair. For beyond the fantasy of control, you are forced to confront the alternative: that some degree of suffering is the inevitable fallout of the human condition. Only when you are willing to let go of your precarious perch do you free yourself from enslavement to the defense of your illusions. This is not your show. What a relief!

Marsha gave her freedom away because she lacked faith in herself and in life. The growth of her associate made the old structure obsolete. In order for her to let him move on, she would have had to trust that something greater than she had yet imagined would take the place of what she had built. Instead, thinking only of the negative possibility of risk, she held on. The price she paid to preserve the illusion of the status quo was the relinquishment of any of the positive potentials brewing in the abyss: the joy of new beginnings, of unexpected directions, of adventure. Whether you choose freedom or preservation, life comes with no guarantees. Your only real choice is whether to live life with fear—or with anticipation.

The most successful real estate investor I know is one who specializes in renovating difficult properties. Before concluding his deals, he goes through the troubled buildings with qualified contractors. He catalogs all the problem areas. Even so, he assumes that no matter how careful he is, after the closing, more will be discovered.

When new problems arise, he feels relieved. His reasoning: he has learned that in anything worthwhile, there are going to be problems. He looks forward to hearing what they are. At least then he knows which problems he's going to be dealing with. The faster he finds out what is wrong, the faster he can correct and move on. While others I know have shipwrecked on the shoals of real estate investing, complaining about how they took a hit on this or that deal, vowing to avoid any of these problems by finding a better deal the next time out, our friend has built a multimillion dollar real estate empire on their rejects.

When you stop wasting energy repressing negative possibilities, you have your complete potential available to you. I got this lesson one disastrous Fourth of July. The plan was that following one last routine client meeting, I would meet my family at the swimming pool of a local hotel for an afternoon of sun and fun. Little did I suspect that this meeting would include their notification of termination of our services. Stumbling out of their office, lost in a fog of remorse, I missed the turn-off to the hotel. By the time I came to, I was an hour's drive farther from my holiday than where I'd started. The long drive back to my family was accompanied by the increasing determination that not only did this failure signify that the business was dying—but I was the one killing it.

I arrived at my family's side, crawling to the pool in utter despair. After hearing my sad story, Dan offered his assurance of faith in me and the business. The children urged me to join them for a frolic in the pool.

I was immobilized. Doomed to failure. How could I ever find my way out of the abyss?

Then, apparently unbidden, I had a tiny, new thought.

What if I could be in despair—and in the pool at the same time! I found a quiet step where I could soak and sulk simultaneously. Before long, the children had engaged me in a splashing contest. Despite myself, the despair could not survive the onslaught of love and laughter.

Surrender came when I understood that, whether my destiny was to succeed or fail in the business, it would come not from squashing or punishing myself, but from being more of who and what I am at any moment. This includes despair as well as joy; moments of genius as well as flat-out failure. Surrendering to this, being able and willing to hold it all at the same time: this is the real source of personal power.

Principle Number Two

In order to become fully successful, you must first be fully alive.

PRINCIPLE NUMBER THREE

*When you empty yourself of the illusions of who
and what you think you are, there is less to lose
than you had feared.*

T HE DEGREE to which you stop protecting yourself from
unpleasant possibilities, emotions and information is the
degree to which you can deal with what is real.

One of my associates runs a nonprofit organization
dedicated to bringing peace to the world. He can rage eloquently
about his desire for world leaders to learn to listen–while not
allowing anyone in his presence to get a word in edgewise. He can
rally for toleration of dissent in the world while exiling his own dis-
sident staff members to organizational Siberia. Everyone who
knows this man admires his results. Few admire his tactics. What
energy he must invest every moment of every day to avoid recognizing in himself the very qualities he has devoted his life to
eliminating in the world!

Can you recognize how much of your career and life are dominated by your desire to avoid seeing things about yourself that are most obvious to others?

You who let glimpses of the truth seep between the cracks of your preferred version of reality begin to experience the most exquisite pain. Your old Gothic constructions may fall apart as the pieces that no longer work for you begin to drift away. Your business may begin to unravel; your current publisher might not like your new project; your boss might choose to fill that position you feel you've earned with someone from outside the organization. Do you grab after these pieces—or do you let them go, trusting that you have the right to a life built on solid ground, not sand?

By admitting how much of your foundation has been built on the unstable ground of illusion, you are freed to take risks. Why? Because when you empty yourself of the illusions of who and what you think you are, there is less to lose than you had feared.

A young seeker travelled across India to find himself seated for tea at the table of a master. The boy extolled his qualifications for disciplehood: his hard work, his accomplishments, his self-discipline and studies. As he talked, the master poured a cup of tea out of a large pot. The boy noticed that the cup was nearly full. Then, the tea began spilling over the cup onto the saucer.

As he continued talking, the boy realized that the master had filled the cup so full, it was now overflowing onto the table and into his lap.

"Master!" the boy exclaimed. "You're spilling the tea!"

The master smiled.

"You are like this cup of tea! So full, there's room for no more. Come to me empty, then we can begin."

With sufficient courage, strength and humility, you can find the willingness to ask questions you have evaded for many years.

Why is it that so many people don't seem to "get" you?

You have an idea of who you think you are. You may even be, like the overflowing teacup, "full of yourself." But who are you, really?

The authority figures in your early years passed along to you survival strategies drawn from their experience of life—experience for the generation that spawned you that included depression, world war and genocide. Coming of age in anxious times, your parents undoubtedly were doing their best to help you navigate the dangerous reefs of survival. The messages many of us got—however loving the motivation on our parents' part—were the product of generations of fear. The result is that our natural faith and wisdom—our authentic perceptions and inclinations—were invalidated over and over again and replaced with principles supplied by outside authority.

Every family has its own secret set of principles, going back through many generations. Perhaps some on this list of commonly held beliefs will be familiar, but your list will be uniquely yours. You were taught, from birth, to swim in your parents' own particular color water. Your acceptance into your first community—upon which your early survival depended—required that you adopt them as your own. In previous chapters, you already explored one of the deep-seated beliefs that you were saddled with from early childhood: "work hard and you will be rewarded."

In a fear-driven culture, you may be honored by your community for the adoption of qualities that are, in reality, the result of obsolete, potentially destructive patterns: the mentor who is celebrated for her generosity while in truth suffering from self-importance, damaging rather than cultivating young talents by forcing them to do it only her way; the self-sacrificing secretary who wins the admiration of her peers for covering up her boss' drinking, thus enabling him to continue his downward spiral.

Do any of these other fear-based principles sound familiar to you?

- Don't trust other people. They will hurt you.
- Fit in at all costs.
- Don't admit problems.
- Imperfection is a sign of weakness.
- Don't seek help. It will leave you vulnerable.
- Introspection is self-indulgent.
- Don't speak the truth about what you feel if it might disturb somebody.
- Expect people to guess what your needs are.
- Asserting divergent desires is disloyalty.
- Judge your friends.

- Get people to do what you want by manipulating them rather than asking them in a straightforward way.
- Value men more than women.
- Covet what other people have. If you can't get it, invalidate it.
- Don't take responsibility for risky ventures; instead, put somebody else in charge, then dump on them if they fail, and hold them responsible.
- Make sure that when you do something good for your community, you are getting recognition and credit for it.

What if your early survival was dependent on adopting principles that, in the long run, are destructive to you? After years of invalidating your own instincts, have these alien principles come to feel safe, familiar and comfortable to you? Could this unhealthy allegiance to a fear-driven system be an addiction, blinding you to the truth? (For more on this addictive system, see the works of John Bradshaw, Anne Wilson Schaef and Alice Miller.)

Addicted to fear-driven principles, you may be suffering from secret guilt coupled with your natural and healthy, but system-threatening, desire to think for yourself. Do you feel ashamed of your desire for faith? Your longing for integrity? Your desire to give and receive love? Your reluctance to crack open this secret box is understandable. As destructive and fear-driven as the principles from which you've been operating your life have been, they've accomplished their goal. What is that? Survival of the status quo.

How do you know they've worked? Because the very fact that you have continued to exist proves it. If you step out of destructive programming to go with values other than what you've been taught, what happens when things get tough? If you try something new, will you survive? Will you turn on yourself as if violating an unstated prohibition?

Who are you, really?

The answer has been hidden, deeply, in the places you are least likely to look: the places where you are ashamed, humiliated or embarassed; where you are brittle and defensive; where you have accused others, fixating on the very qualities in those around you that you most fear finding in yourself.

Dan and I stumbled onto this uncomfortable inner turf in the form of a half-eaten coffee cake. The cake made its fateful appearance on our conference room table early one morning at a time that we felt to be the height of our success as an agency. We had just won our industry's highest national award, a Silver Anvil. Our staff had grown to over twenty people. Despite the foreboding I'd felt upon signing the mortgage papers to our "dream house," we were still living the fast-track lifestyle, looking to all the world like we had it all.

Each and every day, Dan and I led the charge, working sixty and seventy hours a week, expecting our team to do the same. We worked nights. They worked nights. We worked weekends. They worked weekends.

Every week at our staff meeting, Dan and I produced a self-congratulatory coffee cake for our hard-charging award-winning team, settling it on the aforementioned table while regaling them with stories designed to motivate and inspire. The staff would shake their heads, applaud, laugh and nibble.

Thus bonded, we would set them loose to work even harder and longer, setting greater goals, scaling ever higher heights of heady success.

But our weekly staff meeting was held in the afternoon. And this was morning. And this was not our coffee cake.

When we finally mustered the courage to launch an inquiry, our most senior staff member explained that there was growing discontent in the troops. They had gotten together without us—exhausted and resentful—to let off steam.

But what about our staff meetings? Wasn't that their opportunity to tell us how they felt? Week after week, we had watched them bond in teamwork, invigorated by our inspired leadership to set and achieve bigger and bigger goals.

Our staff member looked away sadly, then took a deep breath, gathering courage to proceed.

"Dan, Carol," he said. "Your stories are very inspiring. But that's not why we nod, laugh and applaud."

"It's not?" we breathed equally deeply, gathering courage to respond. "Then why do you do it?"

"We listen to your stories, then do what you ask us to do because we are afraid of losing our jobs."

At that moment, we had a choice. We could have invalidated

our senior staff person's opinion. We could have fired him, and the whole staff for that matter. We could have chosen to ignore the coffee cake and forget the whole thing.

Or we could stop and sneak a peek into the old, dusty, padlocked box that was the place we were most reluctant to look, to see through the illusion of our office camaraderie—our inspired leadership. We could listen and feel for the truth in what was being said to us, and begin the long, arduous task of seeing our part in it, making the corrections that would re-align the reality of our operating assumptions and resulting actions with our stated visions and goals. This was initiation of the process in earnest, the re-evaluation of assumptions we'd taken for granted all of our lives.

Disillusioning as it was, we were willing to surrender to this process based on our growing suspicion that we could only grow towards life-driven business by opening to expanded awareness about ourselves.

Lynn Lumbard, who guides students through the complexities of this process during "Temenos" workshops and meditation retreats, once suggested that her students make a simple shift in their thinking.

"Rather than working to expand your comfort level," she advised, "work to expand your discomfort level."

Discomfort, yes. But how about flat-out pain? The pain, for example, of choosing to consciously deal with a half-eaten coffee cake. Why knowingly choose to experience pain?

I know of only a few people who are brave enough to choose

pain. But I do know increasing numbers of people who choose growth through an expanding awareness of themselves, even knowing that pain may well be the fallout. Why should you do this? Because the alternative is to be unpleasantly surprised over and over again by the damaging results of your unconsciously held assumptions and illusions and the resulting actions and reactions they engender daily in your life.

And also, because as you experiment tentatively at first, then more boldly as your portfolio of growth-oriented experience expands, you are apt to discover a startling new reality. The act of bringing your internal processes into the bright light of day can transform the very issues you have avoided confronting in yourself. The more you open to them, the less you are a victim of them. You open into the pain and hurt, and the wounds have the opportunity to soften and heal. Let it alone, and the pain will work itself out. As incredible as this may sound to the novice, all you have to do is make yourself willing to see. The rest takes care of itself.

Until you have a sufficient data base to know this for yourself, you will need to act on faith. Many of the remaining principles build on the internal skills you are developing to enable you to make this leap of faith. At this point, it is necessary only to empty your teacup. You may sit before the empty cup feeling excitement and anticipation. Or you can sit before the cup feeling hopeless.

All that matters is that your cup be empty. Empty of your illusions. Empty of the fantasy of control. The path to life-driven business asks you to give up a lot. But look at the alternative: what if failure to control the things that happen to you were not the worst possibility? What if the greater tragedy was betrayal of your potential to live life fully?

Like the engineer hanging from the beam, you are already over the edge. What choice have you got?

When your cup is empty, you can proceed on the journey to life-driven business. Only then will you no longer dread being a beginner. You will soon come to realize, with a profound sense of gratitude, that to have begun at all is a miracle.

Principle Number Three

When you empty yourself of the illusions of who and what you think you are, there is less to lose than you had feared.

PRINCIPLE NUMBER FOUR

You have the choice between being the victim of circumstances or being empowered through them.

WHEN WE ARE driven by life rather than by fear, we have faith in the process of our lives, regardless of what our results may seem to be at any given time. Lao Tzu inspired his students with a simple story about a farmer and his horse:

Once there was a farmer whose only possession of merit was a prized horse. All the people in the village ridiculed the farmer.

"Why put all your money into a horse? Somebody could steal the horse and you will have nothing."

The horse did not get stolen. But sadly enough, the horse did run away.

"You fool. You should have diversified—not put so many eggs in one basket. Now you have nothing. You are so unlucky."

The farmer, being a wise man, answered:

THE SEVEN PRINCIPLES OF LIFE-DRIVEN BUSINESS

"Don't say I'm unlucky. Just say that my horse is no longer here. That is a fact. We don't know what may happen next."

Sure enough, the next day the horse returned. And with him was a pack of wild stallions.

The villagers exclaimed, "You were so right! Look how fortunate you are!"

The farmer replied, "You cannot possibly know if this is fortunate or unfortunate. We do not have the whole story yet. Merely say that we got more horses than before."

The farmer set his only son to tame the wild horses. He was thrown and broke his leg. The doctor said he would be crippled for life.

The villagers decried his misfortune but the farmer again asked them to withhold judgment.

Soon thereafter, a war broke out in their country and all the young healthy sons were drafted into battle. Only the farmer's son was left behind. The fighting was fierce and most of the other boys in the village died at war.

"You were right again, farmer," they said.

The farmer shouted, "On and on you go, judging this, judging that. Who do you think you are? How is it that you can presume to know how this is all going to turn out?"

Since we are not in position to judge the ultimate success or failure inherent in the things that happen to us anyway, we can stop wasting valuable energy bribing fate with our good behavior, and get on with it.

When we have given what we can to any particular circumstance, do we get the result we think we want? Or do we let go to embrace instead whatever new directions and experiences circumstances bring to us? Are we able to reap our results now, or are they left to ripen on the vine for some future flowering beyond our current imaginings?

So many of us seem to prefer drama, embellishing our pain with theatrics. We interpret the feelings of fear, sadness, anger or exhaustion as failure. When we are in such a state, thrashing about in the underbelly of our emotions, we overreact, we panic. How badly we've failed! We turn on ourselves, our employees and bosses.

When interviewed by a sportswriter, the coach of a major league baseball team was asked to comment on the chances of bringing up a new, promising pitcher from the minors.

"There is plenty of talent in the minors," he commented. "In fact, some of the boys we have on the farm have stronger skills than the ones we've got here. But the thing is, it's not the talent that is the deciding factor in what makes a major league pitcher."

"What is?" asked the columnist.

"It's how well he learns to fail."

When I think of the successful executives I've represented over the years, I have to agree that it is their ability to fail—rather than their ability to produce a particular product or service—that has made the difference. When they come up on a problem, how fast do they let go of remorse to make the correction and move on? How quickly do they forgive themselves and find the courage to try again?

I spent an exhausting day going after new business for the agency, to no avail. That night, I got together with one of my friends who has always talked about going into business for herself. Instead, she has opted for the security of a government job.

"I've had the worst day!" I shared with her over a round of sushi. "I've just spent the whole day on the phone being rejected."

I expected my friend to commiserate with me, reasserting the validity of her decision to remain in her safe haven. Instead, she looked at me with a surprising degree of envy.

"You've spent all day having people say no to you. But I've spent the whole day saying no to myself."

When you take the drama of self-punishment out of the process, you get to deal with the objective reality of the situation—not just what you fear may be your shortcomings.

The essential difference between being victimized and being empowered is your stubborn refusal to abandon yourself, no matter what comes your way—no matter how inadequate or wrong you fear your responses may be.

Spirituality is not passive. It takes great courage to act on your own behalf—to live your life as if you really matter, mistakes and all. That is what the hero discovers about himself as he faces the dragon. He must dig deep to find new levels of commitment from which to draw. The initiation into these new levels of power comes only when you are willing to face your fear and proceed, anyway.

Outside the business arena, what I fear most is snakes. Imagine my surprise when I took a week-long sabbatical from business, after a particularly exhausting bout with the agency's bottom line, to nurture myself in a meditative surrounding—only to find myself in a desert infested with the biggest rattlesnake crop in decades.

In fact, upon arrival, I was informed that this year, for the first time in anybody's memory, the infamous green rattler, aptly nick-named "seven seconds to heaven," had made its appearance within the retreat boundaries.

Through the weeks of doom and gloom that preceded this long-awaited retreat, I had sustained my efforts with the promise of con-templative hikes through the restorative mountain desert terrain and camping out alone under the stars. Instead, when my moment finally arrived, you would have found me—on those rare occasions I ven-tured outside the safety of my cabin—scurrying along the few paved paths between lodge and dining hall; or worse, frozen in terror as I attempted to discern whether the rattling sound too close for com-fort was a cricket, a water sprinkler or my last seven seconds.

After two or three days, scurrying about the desert chased by my terror, I realized that this was a surprisingly familar feeling. Too familiar. Here it was snakes. At home, it was prospective clients who wouldn't sign on the dotted line when I needed them to.

Then and there, I set my intention to go out into the desert as originally planned. I decided to spend a night on the mountain—from sunset to dawn, regardless of what might come along for me to face—internal or external.

As I walked up the gentle slopes of the high desert foothills, I began my search for a place that felt welcoming and safe. Everywhere I looked, I saw things scurrying. Lizards, beetles. Forget the snakes. I did my best not to think about scorpions, tarantulas, wild pigs, bears and vampire bats.

Seriously committed, I finally found a wash of creamy stones that would do. Spreading out my sleeping bag, I noticed ants the size of grasshoppers. I flicked them away, remembering my vow to stay the night whatever might come my way. Snuggling into the bag, I watched the sunset wash the clouds and the valley below first with shades of pink and apricot, then with deep brown and finally pitch black.

I fell fitfully asleep. Sometime during the night, the full moon having risen high overhead, I awoke suddenly, filled with terror. What was that I heard? Footsteps? A rattler swishing through the brush? I could hear only the beating of my heart and my rapid breaths. I could see nothing with my flashlight. Was this terror merited? What if it was not just my imagination?

I remembered, then, a life-threatening encounter from a decade earlier. Another warm, moonlit night—that time, I had been sleeping in the safety of my own bed. A burglar, looking for

money for drugs, had crawled in through an open window. Grabbing me out of bed, he put a razor to my throat and told me to give
him all my cash.

Instinctively, I led the burglar to a drawer. It was not the drawer
that contained my money; but rather, a sharp pair of scissors. I
wheeled around and thrust it at him. The surprise of my vital
action, more than the strength of my blow, shocked him into
releasing me, and I fled down several flights of stairs to safety.

As I thought of this incident in the light of the full desert
moon, I suddenly understood that my great terror was no less than
the manifestation of my great desire to live.

"Who's there?" I shouted into the desert night, peering into the
full moon's shadows for a glimpse of my destiny. I knew I could run
toward the light of the retreat below, chased by my terror down the
mountainside. But I also knew that if I did that, I would never be
fully empowered. I gathered myself together and proclaimed to
my deepest self: whatever it is that comes to me, I will match and
I will exceed it.

The rustling came closer. What was it this time? In the past, I
had always been spared. There had been other burglars, clients
lost and employees angered, cars had crashed, earthquakes had
rattled, illnesses and debts. And yet, I was given another chance
over and over again.

Stepping out into the moon's shadows, I faced the fear that has
stalked so much of my life. What I saw was the part of me who I

could count on to doubt my competence; who thinks I make stupid choices; who doesn't believe I can make it on my own; who squashes the vitality of others; who thinks I am wasting my life; who thinks other people are better than me; who is reluctant to share her gifts; who spends so much of her life running away from the unknown in terror.

In short, it was all those qualities I most fear about myself that stepped out of the shadows on that moonlit night on the mountain. But, I realized suddenly, I hadn't thought about the snakes, the bats, the clients—or any of the fearful objects that so often fill my consciousness with terror—for many moments. In fact, instead of running across the desert of my consciousness, chased by real or imagined threats, I simply felt sad.

My terrified shadow stepped forward just as the early rays of the morning sun peaked over the mountaintop. And suddenly, I felt an emotion I had not expected to encounter: compassion. I had survived the dark night. And now I could see the woman before me, not only as someone who spent much of her life chased by fear—but as someone who, despite all, had accomplished as much as she had. I realized that every time I pitied myself for my inadequacies, I had been denying the truth: my very willingness to hope for something more out of life, my terror that expressed the urgency of my will to live, my willingness to stretch beyond the boundaries of comfort. I was competent and courageous, too. In the dawn of that special day, I felt magical words form in my heart.

You no longer need to carry the fear of the unknown that has been your legacy. You don't need a wake-up call if you are already awake.

From that moment on, the desert lost its terror for me. Upon returning to work, I knew that my journey from fear to life in the workplace had progressed to the next step. In the following days, as I returned to daily life, with its potential for cruelty, disrespect, abuse, failed results and more, I witnessed my internal process moving to a new stage of empowerment.

When you give up your fascination with how inadequate you've been, how often you've been let down, you begin to understand the magnitude of what it means to live life fully. Giving up the illusion of control, you find comfort in the only place of refuge left: compassion for yourself and for the human condition.

When you can do this, you begin to value, above all, those moments of courage, wisdom and love that demonstrate the nobility we each have, in our earnest efforts to deal with the bittersweet realities of life.

The boss who drops anger mid-rage to acknowledge and apologize for her misdirected emotion; the businessman who brushes himself off from failure to try again; the novelist who supports himself by being a waiter, who replenishes the coffee before your cup is empty; the school teacher who takes a sabbatical, living off her savings, to see if she can launch a new career sharing her thoughts on self-esteem with educators around the country;

the stenographer, afraid of conflict, who walks through his terror to take a recalcitrant client to court to try to collect on services rendered.

You think you know what's best for you—what you really want? But what if the universe doesn't care about the job title you've attained, whether you get the car you think you want, whether you live in the right house in the right suburb, or your kids are in the best school?

What if the universe is interested only in those deeper qualities that ensure the continued evolution of life on our planet? Qualities like character, faith, acceptance and love?

If this were true, you could stop whipping yourself to make your career happen. Instead of pushing and protecting, you would find your real destiny beckoning to you to let it unfold. You keep stuffing your spirit in order to be responsible. But where is your real responsibility? To trust in your own spirit. For the universe cares only about that: that you awaken to your full potential as a life-driven human being.

You can disconnect from the fear of whether you're earning enough points to justify your existence—and learn to trust that regardless of the circumstances in which you find yourself, you can always have the most supreme experience in the world: the experience of being connected to the lifeforce.

The experience of this is reward enough.

I do not live my entire life in this connected state. In fact, for years, I could count on one hand the moments when I was blessed with this experience of deep faith.

There was the time, for instance, when the last of our disgruntled employees left the business, appalled that we were going to try to apply the principles in this book to our business, certain that we would fail.

We had sold our dream home, but the mortgage on the little cottage we planned to move to next had not yet come through. The business was losing money and the *New York Times* had not yet dubbed me the queen of downward mobility. Staying in an inexpensive bed and breakfast, we had surrendered virtually all of our external manifestations.

In a journal entry, I bravely noted:

> I've marched myself to the edge of my experience—living much of my life in tears. When I feel the boundaries expand, I am ecstatic. More and more, I realize that I matter. I do not need to deal pieces of myself away to others—to clients, employees, friends, parents—even my own husband and children.
>
> Never again do I have to let the business consume me. There's more I want to do in my life—more than the business can encompass. Business was never meant to be everything for me. Not my life—but a way to support my life.

This is not a time to listen to old fears–but a time for love and faith. I am okay. We're on the right track. We will get the mortgage on the new house. The business will rebuild into something even more expressive of who I am. I mourn what is passing–but I invest my vital energy into going for what I really want.

And what is that?

To more and more experience how sweetness for no reason at all feels. Walking towards the kitchen to wash the dishes, overwhelmed with gratitude and love. This supremely fulfilling experience is there for all of us all the time: unconditional love for conditional circumstances. This is as good as it gets.

It is easy in the day-to-day theater of life to forget how to feel this deep connection to the lifeforce. In fact, with the great success I experienced following my coronation as queen of downward mobility by the *New York Times*, I took a two-year detour in which I replaced the real experience of inner peace with a poor imitation. There were book deals, national television appearances, film options and speaking engagements. Only when bigger, better, and increasingly exciting opportunities stopped pouring in did I realize that I had, once again, accepted an impersonation of success, although it was a good one.

Writing this book, I am again in a career transition. As my desire to devote more of my time to writing and teaching comes forward, my part of the business is reforming itself in size and style, yet again. The question for me comes down to a simple equation: will my new vision reconstitute into sufficient livelihood to support my current lifestyle faster than the manifestation of the old vision recedes? The *I Ching* consoles me, reminding me to refrain from over-investing in the old reality that is dropping away.

While it is natural to feel anxiety and sadness as I say goodbye to the old, comfortable ways that have brought me to this place, I must discipline myself to also recognize the excitement inherent in the new ways that are birthing.

The challenge is in being able to hold everything at the same time, including the pain of having to make tough choices, leaving aspects of myself that have been important to me behind.

We can forgive ourselves for the mistakes we've made—for turning against ourselves. Did we lose the perspective of the magnitude of the task we had taken upon ourselves? Of course we have insecurities about our motivation, our ability, our strength, our sincerity. These doubts are the universe's forge, strengthening the metal of our character with courage. We confront the truth about our whole selves, the strengths as well as weaknesses. Not as a child who proclaims, "Here is my authentic self: you have to love it."

No, we must learn to say simply, "Here I am, flaws and all. While I would prefer your respect, I am willing to take the consequences."

We know we have progressed in our journey to life-driven

business when we recognize that we would rather have the pain of consciousness than forfeit authentic experience. To be authentic, we must be willing to walk alone. Ironically, only when the passion of our inner journey takes precedence over what others might think, do we have a self who is fully available to give and receive love.

It is as if, on some level, I am back at the bed and breakfast, between houses. This time, however, I have the memory of the road that brought me here. What I learned last time is that I could not afford to wait for the circumstances of my life to bring me the experience of success. I had to learn to generate the warm feelings I associated with success first . . . without regard for the outcome. It is with the development of my character and spirit, not my results, that my loyalty lies.

You can become so enthralled with the unfolding process of your own authenticity—and of those around you—you may well forget what it was you thought you wanted to accomplish in the first place. If you are among the few who are courageous enough to acquire an appreciation for life's complexities, you will never run out of fascinating material. The ultimate gift is not that you will get what you think you want; but that you can come to genuinely appreciate what you get.

Here in the twilight of the twentieth century, we suffer from the pretense that we have tamed the universe. We forget that when we surrender, it is not to a perfect conception of order and peace. We find spirit, rather, by surrendering to the full range of possibilities.

The Zen master tells this story:

A man was riding in the back of an ambulance, in great pain.

"God," he prayed. "God—please take away my pain."

The man hears a resonant voice.

"But I just gave you the pain," answers God.

Is there a divine plan? Only that you rise out of the daze you have effected in the name of control and safety, awakening to become what the universe intends you to be: a whole, integrated human being.

Principle Number Four

You have the choice between being the victim of circumstances or being empowered through them.

PRINCIPLE NUMBER FIVE

When you are driven by life,
the odds will be with you.

I F THESE PRINCIPLES were simply a matter of showing the way to surrender, it would be enough. In having come just this far, you would find yourself more willing and more able to trade your illusions for a newfound grasp on reality. You would have expanded clarity and awareness of yourself and others. Out of this, you will manage your careers and business more effectively: you will make better decisions based on a better grasp of the facts.

But I believe there's much more. When you are courageous enough to challenge your beliefs to take up the task of being fully alive, you create an increased opportunity for forces beyond your comprehension to become engaged in your success.

Does this sound irrational? There are many things that happen every day that defy rational explanation: spontaneous remission of illness; premonition of news; coincidence; intuition; "luck."

Think of the businessman who, on the brink of bankruptcy, prays for deliverance and the phone rings with a big chunk of work; or the graphic artist, stuck for creative direction, who stumbles across inspiration while thumbing through old magazines in the reception room of the dentist's office. Remember when a crisis turned out for the best in your life: Perhaps you got rejected from law school, loved your "interim" job working in a pet hospital and ended up becoming a veterinarian.

Once upon a time, eclipses, rainstorms, gravity and fire were not understandable in terms of existing science. Over millennia, each was incorporated into rational understanding. Lightning has been harnassed. The rest have been explained by laws of physics and chemistry. As we begin the transition from one millennium to another, who is to say whether those things that you now consider "irrational" won't someday also be explained by some known—or yet to be discovered—law? What that law will be, THAT it will be, is as irrelevent today to the fact that these things exist, as is understanding how or why electricity works to using an electric light. You would be foolish to wait for someone to scientifically prove that there is some force working on your behalf in the universe before you began to trust your intuitive experience.

You need only to observe nature over time to see that actions that promote life have a greater tendency to succeed than those that promote the suppression of life. Beginning with our biology, we count the improbable odds of fertilization of a single egg by a single sperm. New life begins with the release of billions of sperms into a hostile environment, driven by mysterious forces, competing amongst themselves, to reach the goal of fertilization. Only one will succeed. That elemental triumph is the foundation of your existence.

Each of you has this expression of lifeforce as your personal legacy. The very fact that you have come into existence is miraculous.

The universe can be counted on to support new growth. What is born, over time, has always exceeded that which passes away. Think of our prehistory and the ability of man to survive the perils of nature; or our current history and the continuation of civilization despite the access to unprecedented tools of destruction: the presence of life on this planet is a miracle.

You carry within you the inheritance of this miracle: a lifeforce that follows a continuous thread of existence back to the very beginning of time — into the very heart of the deepest mysteries of the universe. As a link in the chain that finds both its roots and its destiny in the unknown, you are entrusted in this particular time and place with a sacred responsibility. You are no less than the embodiment of lifeforce: you are not its source, but rather, the most contemporary vehicle of its expression.

Having spent time presenting proposals to various clients over the years, I witnessed in myself and my staff a curious phenomenon. On any given day, any one of us could be counted on to present our material, informing or educating audiences in a professional manner. But for the majority of us, there can come a moment when we transcend performance to merge with the material. On the cherished occasions when I have felt this energy, I have not only influenced those in my presence, I have moved them.

Actors, professional speakers, musicians and the like are perhaps more aware than the rest of us of this connection. They actively create the space, the environment, the receptivity for lifeforce to manifest through them. I know one speaker who, prior to every lecture, visualizes white light moving from the universe through the top of her head and out into the audience.

When I am going into an important presentation, feeling anxious or insecure, I have learned from her to take a moment to tap into a source of motivation greater than my self-will.

There is an ancient Chinese story that illustrates this point. A small village was suffering from a devastating drought. A rainmaker was summoned to perform a magical ritual. When he arrived, he said he would not be able to begin for some time. He asked for a hut away from the village and five days of food. On the fourth day, it began to rain. The villagers rushed to his hut to thank him. But the rainmaker protested that he had not done the ceremony yet.

When he arrived in the village, he explained, he had felt that he was not right with himself. He had spent the time trying to regain balance and integrity. Such was the power of his commitment, the rectification of his internal process swept along the rectification of the climate in its wake.

We are all capable of channeling this vital energy. The more you clear out the stress and effort associated with the illusions and false assumptions addressed in the previous chapters, the more receptive you are to the manifestation of the lifeforce as you go about your daily activities.

If you program your internal computer with this new belief, you can start swimming with, rather than against, the current by managing your career, business and life as if your well-being, and the well-being of those who report to and work with you matter. When your actions are consistent with the lifeforce, you experience the spontaneous support of the universe. Rather than feel that the more you do, the farther behind you fall, you feel that for every small step you take, you move a yard.

I had the good fortune of experiencing this principle in action not long after the agency moved our office to San Francisco's Union Street. The street of boutique shops is famous as the place to go for many of the world's most precious gift items. But when we moved our offices there, we soon discovered what was to be the rarest and most sought after of its many offerings: a parking space.

Our lease included one. I should have guessed what lay in store for me when the landlord's fine print included the disclaimer that he would not be responsible for the towing of trespassers.

To get to this parking space, you must first know that the crack between two Victorian buildings, which looks as if it might be left over from the Great Quake of '06, is actually an alley leading to a private parking lot. Once you position your vehicle for entry, you ease between the walls, careful to avoid the wooden post at the corner that has been scraped so often you can see the whorls that were growing when Columbus discovered America.

Then, if you are lucky, all you need to do is remove a crate or a couple of bags of vegetable matter overflowing from the garbage dumpster that shares your space, to make room for your car. To enter, you wildly crank the steering wheel right and then left, timing the release of the brake and the application of gas in a complex synthesis of discipline and motion.

I soon came to realize that renting a private parking space anywhere in the vicinity of Union Street is somewhat akin to buying the deed to the Brooklyn Bridge.

Every time I pulled down the skinny alley to this troubled parking space, it was occupied. If it wasn't the guy who owned the shop next door, unloading bare boughs for his winter window display, it was a friend of one of the apartment dwellers nearby. There were messengers, loan applicants, shoppers, diners, drinkers and women with ragged nails desperate to make their appointment with their manicurist.

How they even found the space was astonishing, but that they braved our increasing collection of threatening signs–"Unauthorized Vehicles Will Be Towed" and "Do Not Even Think of Parking Here"–was a miracle.

I learned to herald my arrival with angry honks. Often the guilty party could be summoned thusly, attuned to the abrasive sound like a dog to a whistle. Fueled by righteous anger, my blood and tongue would race. With fist shaking, I'd watch as they'd angle back and forth, frantic for escape, finally clearing the way and racing to freedom.

Whatever triumph I felt through this primitive exchange was offset by the residue of anger that, once released, refused to depart.

Then there was the day, car poised for entry, when I was unwilling to go through this drama one single more time. Preparing to beat my chest, I instead found myself taking a small but decisive step on behalf of the evolution of mankind. As I thought of the press of humanity, questing for nothing more than my chunk of concrete under the sun, I stopped fighting and, instead, made an internal offering.

Anger hadn't worked. What if I blessed them? Wished to those less fortunate than I that they get exactly what they want in their lives. Surely, I did not want the woman with ragged nails to miss her appointment, the messenger to be unable to deliver his packages.

Yes, I do want them to get what they want. But, of course, I preferred if they could get it in some other way than inconveniencing me. If that was not possible, however, I would give them my space as a gift. There would be other battles worth fighting, I knew. I would from this point on pick my battles more carefully.

There have, indeed, been other battles. But rarely have they been about where to park my car. Because since that day, the space has rarely been unlawfully occupied. Each time I round the corner into the crack, I re-create once more the willingness to surrender my will, no matter what the cost to me personally, and more often than not, I find the open space, welcoming me.

I have applied the same basic principle of surrender to everything from hiring employees to getting new accounts.

During the 1991 war with Iraq, the agency's new business skidded to a halt. Despite our massive outreach to new clients, our business climate was basically on hold for two months. Our associate Harvey Bailey, bemoaning the problems that had beset his agency, commented that he understood the reluctance of potential clients to sign on the dotted line.

"I'm so insecure about the future of the world, I'm afraid to make any commitment longer-term than ordering a piece of pie," Harvey offered.

Hitting the phones every day, Dan and I realized that we were on the fast track to burnout. Rather than continue to push upstream, we decided to take a different approach. We would follow up responsibly with those prospects who had indicated interest. But beyond that, we would take our vital energy and invest it in whatever channels remained open to us. We spent more time with our family, healing and nurturing our little unit. We took special care of ourselves, taking time to meditate and to record our thoughts and emotions in our journals. If you had asked us what we were doing about new business during this period, we would have answered honestly, "we prayed a lot."

The day the war ended, the phone started ringing. We believed that fate would complete its cycle of misfortune: sooner or later, it always does. And it did. By using the time of uncertainty to revitalize and nurture ourselves and those around us, we emerged from the crisis with our spirits intact. There was a pent-up demand for our services and we were ready, able and willing to rise to the occasion.

When I gave an early version of this manuscript to one of my clients, he simply could not buy the concept that when you are driven by life, the odds will be with you. A hard-driving insurance executive, Sam fervently believed that he had achieved his lofty success through commitment, effort and willpower.

"I've worked hard for everything—and it hasn't been easy," he explained to me in the back seat of his limousine on the way back from an interview with an important business publication. Accompanying us on our ride that day were his raging ulcer and a pronounced nervous tic.

Sam pulled out what he considered to be the secret of his success. It was a carefully crafted chart, in which every twenty-four-hour day of the week was divided into fifteen-minute segments. Using brightly colored felt tip pens, he had designated red blocks for meeting with his subordinates; massive amounts of purple were destined for meetings with current and potential clients. There were huge swatches of yellow, black and orange.

"What's that little bit of green?" I asked, pointing to a slender stripe across the bottom of the page.

"That's time for family, fun and relaxation."

As we turned the corner to my office, I asked him why he had such a problem with the concepts in this book.

"It's not that I don't see where you're coming from," he replied. "It's just that while it may be true that the universe wants you to succeed—it sure as heck doesn't necessarily want me to succeed."

In that moment, I had an inspiration.

"What if," I boldly ventured "it wasn't your willpower that got you your results? What if your results came despite your willpower?"

"You may be right," he said finally. "But I am not willing to pay the price of finding out that I am the exception to your rule." Popping Maalox, his eye twitching beneath its accumulation of stress, Sam rode off into his next swatch of red.

Sam is far from alone. Receiving an invitation to address several hundred men and women at a Chamber of Commerce function in the Midwest, I agonized over how to take my talk onto the new terrain I'd been forging with this book. How could I convince a roomful of potential Sams to at least consider the possibility that there could be a positive connection between spirituality and success?

When I discussed this challenge with Dan, he proposed that I point out that each one of them undoubtedly had on their person, that very day, the symbolic representation of this radical new concept.

"You must be kidding," I replied.

Then Dan reached into his pocket and pulled out a well-worn dollar bill.

"Annuit Coeptis," he read aloud. "Latin for 'He looks with favor upon our undertaking.'"

Did our forefathers share my belief that the universe really does want us to succeed?

Research led me to Dr. Willis Harman's book, *Global Mind Change* (Knowledge Systems Inc., 1988). He points out that the design of the dollar bill was set in 1782. The symbolism derives from the transcendental philosophy of Freemasonry. In fact, fifty of the fifty-six signers of the Declaration of Independence, including Benjamin Franklin and George Washington, were Masons. The roots of our economic system hail back to these potent images, clearly drawing the connection between spiritual principles and economic success.

The Great Seal of the United States of America, for example, features an unfinished pyramid topped by the omnipotent eye of the universe. I interpret this to mean that while we can accomplish much on our own, our work is incomplete unless inspired by a power greater than ourselves. Beneath the pyramid are the words of Virgil: "Novus Ordo Seclorum" or "A new order of the ages is born."

As I strode on-stage that night, dollar bill firmly clenched in hand, my ideas no longer seemed so radical. Our entire economic system was based on images that bore a striking resemblance to the same thoughts that Sam found so incredulous. Is this "new order" none other than the "new paradigm" that today's organizational transformation consultants are bringing to our forward thinking corporations? That Stephen Covey writes about in his best-selling book? That is making it possible, at long last, for a book like this one to be sold not only in new age, philosophical, or religious specialty stores, but in the business section of mainstream bookstores?

Imagine how you would relate to your career, business and life if you chose to adopt the irrational belief I share with our forefathers—that this is a universe that wants you to prosper. What if you made your decisions based on your faith that the universe does not judge you on the results of your life to date? What if the universe does not need evidence from you that your existence is justified? What if you have been forgiven for the sacrifices you have failed to make; the goals you have not yet achieved? Imagine how you would feel if you knew that life accepts you unconditionally no matter what you do?

Would it really matter whether or not you could replicate these theories in a scientific laboratory? Maybe I can't prove to you that the universe wants you to succeed—but can you prove to me that it doesn't? Not even the greatest scientist of our time can know something as basic as when time began; or where the outer boundaries of the universe may be found. How can you be so sure of your beliefs?

What I longed to explain to Sam is that the miracles I had been experiencing in the transformation of my own career and business did not come just from my loving life—but from life loving me.

I approach every day believing that whatever happens to me is evidence of the universe's support of my growth and development as a human being. Of course, you may say, the stakes of faith when it comes to the delivery of a parking space are relatively low. How about when you get fired from your job, or blow a critical opportunity? Will you feel the universe's love and support of you then?

Principle Number Five

When you are driven by life, the odds will be with you.

PRINCIPLE NUMBER SIX

Your ordinary self is enough.

INSPIRED BY a Zen teaching, I have my own version of the story of the secretary of a real estate developer who was attending a national convention. The secretary with the company of a competing developer happened by.

"My boss can build cities in three different countries simultaneously. What miraculous things can your boss do?" the competitive secretary asked.

"Only this," said the first. "When he's hungry, he eats. When he's tired, he sleeps."

When you are living life fully, you are not doing something you think of as great. You are merely doing what's next. You are not pushed at a self-destructive pace by fear. Turning a deaf ear to the sirens of false promise, you no longer work so intensely that you

and with the explosion of creativity came an outpouring from the collective unconscious that is the basis of Jungian psychology.

Sometimes you will be inspired, sometimes you will feel lost. You will make mistakes along the way and you will learn from your mistakes. Even this you won't do perfectly.

Over the past twenty years, I have monitored the progress of one of my friends, one of the Bay Area's premiere bakers. I first sampled his claim to fame—a rich cheesecake based on an old family recipe—at a potluck party. I'm sure I was one of the many people who said to him, "You really should do something with this." I watched him progress as a patron and sometimes public relations agent to his fledgling, and then fast growing chain of bakeries. At one point, he experimented with democratic management—to nearly disastrous effect. New products made bold debuts then quietly slipped away into oblivion. Some locations worked. Some didn't. The corporation's numbers slipped, slid and soared depending on the season, the personnel and a hundred other factors. But through it all, he held his center. His chain of bakeries is now a multimillion dollar empire. To him, and to all those who have brought this kind of life-driven spirit to their work, I dedicate this prayer.

PRAYER FOR LIFE-DRIVEN BUSINESS

Help me to give up pushing, demanding and desiring
specific rewards from my work. I trust that I am being led to

my greater purpose the fastest possible way. The job I am doing now is a small part of what you have in store for me. The real purpose of my work is to provide a forum for the evolution of my spirit, my emotion, my strength, and my power.

If it seems long and difficult at times, it is because I am a beginner and there is so much to learn. If I feel restless, impatient and frustrated at the pace of the process, at the apparent setbacks, I trust that I am evolving the fastest, most direct way. If I am disappointed along the way, without anger, self-hatred or judgment, I simply make whatever corrections I can. If I can't find anything to correct, or if I have reached the point where to give more will sacrifice my overall vitality and well-being, I have the patience to wait.

When I am tempted to take a short-cut I know does not come from my own desire for integrity, grant me the clarity to see that a fast, forced imitation will merely give the illusion of success.

I ask you to help me love myself, wherever I am in the process, trusting that I am always doing my best—given where I've come from, and the circumstances I face. When I compare myself to others, I will turn jealousy into a blessing for them, feeling grateful for what I, too, have achieved. When I am faced with deprivation or disappointment—in myself or fate—I will transform anger into gratitude for the daily practice that you have given me in the form of my job—a practice that I trust will provide me with the specific means of strengthening my spirit for the unfolding of the greater purpose you have set forth for me.

On one of my media tours, I was met at the airport by one of the producers of a national cable program, operating outside of Washington D.C. I was struck by the serenity of my hostess. My awe increased as she told me that she had just recently discovered that the funding for the program had fallen short and that she was on the final day of her job with no new opportunity yet in sight.

"When I came here several years ago, I wanted to break into broadcast more than anything in the world. I loaded all my belongings into my VW and pulled into town. I was down to my last dollar, but I trusted that something would happen for me."

Indeed, she got the job offer within days.

Now, several years later, she was dropping me off at the studio—her last task before going home to pack her bags.

"How can you be so composed at a time like this?" I asked.

"Simple. When I first heard about problems here, I started praying. I let the universe know that my preference—given my limited perspective—was to stay in this job. But I also asked that if this were not what I am meant to do, that the door be closed."

She explained to me that in her life, every time a door closed, sooner or later, another door opened. Sometimes, even by her own admission, the timing of doors slamming shut and others cracking open was less than ideal. She felt that it was in those difficult transitional periods that she did the most growing.

Even as I listened, I tempered my awe of her with the quiet suspicion that her faith was derived mainly from an insufficient data base. As the older, more experienced, battle-worn woman I imagined myself to be, I came away wondering if the key to her serenity was that she was young and privileged enough to not have had to experience real pain yet. While I aspire to the sweet simplicity of her trust, I have not been able to solve the riddle of how to be more fully conscious—without also being more fully afraid.

Following the principles shared in this book, I have come face to face with feelings and emotions that I was once able to avoid through external diversion. These feelings no longer lurk secretly in my unconscious, programming my internal computer to respond with actions and points of view that are not always in my long-term best interest.

Accessible to me, exposed in the bright light of day, my fears are more apparent to me now than ever before. *But they drive me less.*

Who among us, awakened from the once comforting illusions that no longer suffice, would not feel trepidation? I have learned that I cannot always count on the serenity of faith to save me from my fears. Perhaps the best I can hope for is to be able to name my terror and be willing to rise to the occasion. The real challenge, in fact, may be not to avoid fear, but rather to extend acceptance to myself even when I am afraid. There is an elegance and simplicity about this process, uncomfortable as it may at times be.

If you can find self-acceptance no matter what you feel or do, and if things will go wrong no matter how good you are, ask yourself: what's the hurry? Why suffer relentless pressure to achieve and accomplish if you cannot judge your success or failure by looking at your results and manifestations at any given time?

To exist in life without using your ability to impress others in the redundant effort to justify your right to a good life: this is the source of success that can sustain the vicissitudes of fate. You no longer need to show how deserving you are of success. You are already good enough—whatever the circumstances in which you find yourself at the moment.

Legend has it that Alexander the Great once came upon a saint, sunning himself on the bank of a river.

"Old man, you look so content. What I would give to be able to sit there like you and enjoy the sun!" said Alexander.

The saint laughed, asking Alexander where he was headed.

"I have one last battle to fight. Then I will come back and join you!" he replied.

"You foolish man," said the saint. "Why go to conquer yet another people when all you want to do in the end is sit here in the sun and rest? I've conquered no one. Send your armies home and sit beside me now and enjoy the day."

Alexander spurned the invitation, marching off to what turned out to be his final encounter. He died on the battlefield.

How many of you are putting off your moment in the sun until you get it right? When you just get that stack of papers cleared off your desk; when you land that next client or job? You have things you have to and want to do. When you empty your in-basket, you're high. When it fills up again, you're low. But can you, instead, let your life happen all of the time? Full or empty? In success or failure?

When you have this perspective, what is happening to you at any particular moment loses so much of its significance. You see the bigger picture. As a boss, I see that one of the primary strengths I am developing is my ability to hold this bigger picture for my employees when they have lost it for themselves.

Arriving at the office one Monday morning, I discovered a flurry of press releases, soiled coffee cups, and scratch paper strewn wildly about. Something had happened between the time I left early Friday afternoon and my arrival three days later. In fact, a case settlement had come in for one of our law clients, representing a major food company.

The team assigned to the account had dropped everything to get a release out in a timely manner. Enthused by the challenge, they had risen to the occasion gloriously. Placements were running in legal and general news media publications even as I spoke about it with them that Monday.

As is the informal policy of the agency, I suggested that they take comp time to allow themselves to recover and revitalize after their extraordinary effort. Surely other, less stressed staff members could take up the slack. But running on the adrenaline of success, they turned down the offer.

Toward the end of the week, I saw the senior account executive sitting at his computer, holding his head. He had a migraine headache.

"Why don't you go home and take a rest?" I suggested.

"Because I'm already falling behind. If I leave now, I'll lose even more ground. In fact, we're making plans to come in again this weekend."

Drawing on the wisdom of twenty years of business, I knew that this team's health and vitality were worth far more to me and their client than whatever they felt they could accomplish in an extra day or so. Great employees get sick, go on vacation, get called on jury duty, and the business survives. The business could survive their weekend off, too.

The senior account executive pulled up his "to do" list on the computer screen, proof in black and gray that he had read the crisis correctly. But before I would mark it off with him, I asked a favor. Pressing a couple of dollars into his palm, I asked him to take a long walk and take time to sip an even longer espresso. If upon his return he still felt he needed to work non-stop through another weekend, we could revisit the issue then.

He not only walked to the espresso place, he walked all the way to the bay. Watching the waves roll in and roll out for an hour or so, he later reported to me that the city seemed so small and far away. As his headache subsided, he began to see that he had geared himself and his team up to a fever pitch. He was on a battle high–exploring the outer limits of his ability to dominate and control.

Upon his return, he looked at the blinking computer screen with fresh eyes. As it turned out, many items on the list could wait until next week. The few that needed immediate attention were less time-consuming than he'd feared, and of those few, some could be delegated to other staff members who had the time and willingness. He was out by five for a well-earned, long and guilt-free weekend.

The simpler the life, the easier it is for us to avoid distractions from what we really want. The effort to control destiny no longer compels us to action. When we are stressed, anxious, confused, we have the option of ceasing to push against our limitations and wait.

When we are no longer driven to be extraordinary, we know that things are not as serious as they seem. Once we understand this principle we will feel no need to be driven to extremes. We can learn to laugh at ourselves and all of our significance.

When we do this, we begin to manage the people and the events we encounter with a lighter but more effective touch.

In place of the pressure to achieve, we can find it in our repertoire to simply do nothing, acting again only when we trust ourselves to set a pace that is chosen out of life rather than fear. This is the discipline recovering overachievers truly need: to cut ourselves some slack.

Going through a particularly rough January at the agency, I got together with a friend in the high-pressure custom clothing business, who is as wise as she is successful. I described to her that every January since I could remember, I dreaded the feeling that I was having to pay for my time off during the holidays by "getting serious" and "making it happen." I was pushing myself to function as best I could under the circumstance—day after day. But the effort to perform was getting more and more unbearable.

She had an alarmingly simple solution.

"The next time you approach the office, ask yourself how you are feeling. If you feel fine, proceed. If you are freaking out, don't go in."

She told me that she had once stood on the curb across the street from her store for over an hour, overwhelmed by the challenges she faced—not knowing where to begin. As she stood, she gave herself permission to feel upset without the added judgment that it meant anything about her ability to do her job.

While she was giving herself permission to have feelings, she found herself wondering whether an important call she'd been waiting for had come in yet. She daydreamed about a certain sleeve that she felt the urge to sketch. She recognized that the combination of fabrics she saw on a woman as she passed by presented a simple solution for one of the knottier challenges she faced. She practically ran across the street to work.

When you stop pushing, "doing nothing" turns out not to be

lost time. Its value is not only recuperative—although that would be benefit enough. By emptying yourself of fear-driven effort, you make the space to receive information, insight and creative solutions not available through action-oriented behavior.

You stop beating down your potential for big, juicy ideas with avalanches of reactive little thoughts. You take the time to ponder, to appreciate, to daydream. When you have faith, you can choose when and how to let go of your rational processes—to let the intuitive spirit have its moment. You surrender the arrogance of your controlled intellect to bask patiently in the world of obscured images, plans and knowledge pressing, as if of their own accord, to take shape.

Even the Japanese, whose proclivity for long hours at work resulted in the modern tragedy of *karoshi*, honor the value of daydreaming in the context of the workday. In most American offices, if a worker is seen to be staring blankly out the window, the boss is apt to assume the worker is either slacking off, or hasn't been given enough to do. In Japan, however, the daydreamer is left alone. His time sitting quietly with himself is treated with honor and respect.

In their autobiographies, western tycoons often brag about the intensity with which they work. Not only do they set a breakneck pace throughout the day, but many report cutting back their hours of sleep to as few as possible. As effective as these tycoons may be, they are cheating themselves and the world of their freest, wildest and potentially most productive creativity—access to the unconscious that does not even occur when they are awake.

Sleeping is not wasted time. Your dreams overflow with visual puns, clever juxtapositions and symbolism. Are these unconscious manifestations accidental? Are your dreams, as some scientists believe, the result of an overworked machine-like organism called the brain discharging random electrical impulses that have no meaning?

Or, could your dreams be a crack through which you may peek into the inner universe—a way for you to access information from the unconscious to reveal the real issues of your life—your own personal dragons you have yet to slay.

A story about an associate of mine demonstrates how effective dreams can be in providing practical information critical to making good decisions. Remember the "inspirational" story of the "Chicken and the Pig?" One of the managers of the restaurant chain I wrote about in the beginning of this book was deeply upset with the death of her fellow worker. Soon after his funeral, she called and asked if we could go for lunch. The corporate culture of the chain had made working nights and weekends the rule rather than the exception. A graduate of Cornell, she knew she was on the track to the kind of success in her field she had always envisioned. But she had just broken up with a boyfriend who felt strongly that she had the right to take time to have a life outside the corporation. Even though they had parted ways, rumors persisted about her lack of seriousness and commitment to the company in light of her outside social life.

Upset and confused, she started therapy. After a number of sessions, she suddenly came to know—without a doubt—that she needed to leave her position, no matter what the cost appeared to be to her career in the short-term. She had sought me out on this occasion to discuss career opportunities in the field of public relations.

Such a dramatic and courageous career change! How, I asked her, had she come to such certainty that she was doing the right thing?

The answer had come to her in the form of a dream, worked through with the help of her therapist. In the dream, Stan (the owner of the chain of restaurants) lured her into his private office. As long as she resisted, he proceeded with seduction. But the moment she surrendered, the seduction turned into a brutal rape. Since Stan is an attractive, virile man, my friend had suggested to the analyst that, unbeknownst to her conscious self, she must have been harboring unresolved sexual feelings for her boss which were complicating her decision-making process.

"As we explored the feelings that the dream elicited in me, I realized that my intellectual interpretation of the dream was not ringing true. It became apparent that Stan was the archetypal symbol for my ambition—the ambivalence I feel about the seduction of the supposedly glamorous career path I'd chosen. The dream let me know in no uncertain terms that surrender to all that Stan represents violated my most deeply held values and needs."

She began her new career search the next day.

In the survey response to the Inner Excellence Bulletin, executives in companies across the United States reported a variety of ways they use to gain access to their inner wisdom. We mentioned long walks, espresso and dreams. But the possibilities are endless.

A publishing company in Alabama has set aside an office for employees to take an afternoon nap. The CEO of a computer company in Boston consults the tarot before making important decisions. When a salesman in Portland, Oregon, realizes that he is becoming overinvested in his results, he puts the phone down and, instead of calling on prospects, does crossword puzzles.

Cultivating entry into the irrational world of the unconscious lifeforce is a patient process, requiring utmost gentleness. For your greatest inspirations and insights are like the most tender sprouts: they simply cannot push up through the concrete of the busy edifices that comprise your daily routine.

You must learn to tend your inner garden, not only in the harvest of the fall; but through the long, empty winter, when you are called upon to invest faith in meditations, in contemplation, in dreams that do not seem to make any sense, in unformed feelings that make you restless, in yearnings that have no object and no names. When you let go of your rational, ordinary routines, you discover that your efforts to control reality had, in actuality, limited your options. You gain access to wisdom, perspective, and knowledge that could never come from tugging at your rational mind.

Soon after taking the reins of Apple Computer, CEO John Sculley shocked the computer industry by taking off on a sabbatical. Beginning in 1985, Apple allowed any employee with five years' experience to take up to six weeks sabbatical with full pay. Sculley decided to take not only his six weeks, but added three weeks of vacation to it.

He took off for his ranch in Maine where he designed a barn and took a photography class. He returned with plans to streamline management, doing away with many of the company's routine meetings. Credited with much of that company's success at that time, he quadrupled Apple's revenues to over $4 billion.

When you give up the need to make things happen—making demands on life to give you what you think you deserve—you open space for possibilities to arise from outside your ordinary experience and expectations. This is my definition of a miracle.

Principle Number Six

Your ordinary self is enough.

PRINCIPLE NUMBER SEVEN

*To achieve greatness,
you must be willing to surrender ambition.*

WHEN YOU are fully alive, you are not trying to make it, nor are you trying not to make it. There is nothing to prove. So why do anything? Certainly not just for the payoff at the end but for the satisfaction of the process. Making it is no longer the criterion for success. It is a by-product—what happens along the way while you are living your life. You set goals, but you aren't driven by them. You give these goals everything you've got, understanding that "everything" includes taking time to nurture yourself at a pace supportive of your overall vitality. If this is what you choose to do with your newfound freedom, you will not only find that you have sufficient energy to take care of yourself—but you will have enough left over to share with others. You no longer approach every opportunity by asking what you can get; instead you discover more opportunities to give.

According to Chinese tradition, Lao Tzu's disciples were travelling through a forest one day where hundreds of trees had been cleared. In the center was one huge tree with hundreds of branches. Woodcutters rested in its shade.

The disciples asked the woodcutters why the tree had been left standing.

"Because it is absolutely useless. The bark is so tough, it breaks our saws. And even if we are able to chop off a piece, the smoke it makes when burned stings our eyes."

When the disciples reported this conversation to Lao Tzu, he laughed.

"Be like this tree. Be absolutely useless. If you become useful, somebody will come along and make a chair out of you. Be like this tree and you will be left alone to grow big and full, and thousands of people will come to rest under your shade."

When you make a commitment to living life fully, you clear away reactive, fear-driven motivation and uncover the roots of your own authentic vitality. Being inspired is your natural state. Your vitality evolves every time you give yourself permission to pay attention to the deep-rooted things you care about. This deep attunement is the natural source of enthusiasm, a word that in its original Greek form means "to be filled with God."

When you are fully alive, you do not need to push or prod yourself and those around you to function up to their potential. You have no more need of ambition than does a plant's new growth, bursting through the soil towards light.

In this principle, you find the only cure for judging yourself on the basis of achievement. Approval from others, rewards and judgments become irrelevent. You no longer worry if you are wasting your time or if you will be successful. Your energy is freed to express and to create.

How this will manifest may look very different from time to time in the span of a single life. Your life will likely take unpredictable new turns. There will be adventure and surprises.

You may recognize that you've been hiding out in an outgrown career or business, and courageously choose to take a well-earned time-out to pursue something as privately passionate as planting a vegetable garden and watching the seeds grow. On the other hand, you may recognize that you've beaten a retreat to spiritual pursuits as a safe refuge from which to avoid dealing with fears of failure, and re-enter the world with renewed power and passion.

Some of you will find the shedding of old stable structures liberating. Others will find the willingness to settle down at last to be life's greatest adventure. You may discover within you a deep caring about the planet and the people on it, giving altruistic activities precedence over your history of self-serving motivation. Or you may discover that your apparently deep caring about the planet and the people on it was motivated by a desire for personal power and manipulation, not the altruistic motivations you wished to be known for.

Ironically, espousing high aspirations and ideals for yourself and the world are no guarantee that you are an evolved manifestation of the lifeforce. Every June, I am deluged by resumés from young people who believe it is their destiny to change the world. When you are in your early twenties, it is probably healthy to hold the point of view that you are specially destined to make an important contribution to humanity. Be it from arrogance or fear, greed or grandiosity, the result is that businesses are founded, careers are launched, community organizations get grants, books are written, funds get raised.

But many a "good" person who sets out to help others, to share their many offerings, to change the world for the better, has held a position of moral superiority, replacing authentic inspiration with the inner conviction that they are more deserving than others of the universe's support and recognition.

I played the role of both the winner and the loser in one such reckless negotiation with fate for twenty years. In fact, the story I will share with you—including the most acute instances of both pain and glee during my coming into adulthood—is finally moving beyond the drama of reward and punishment, taking on the larger perspective of a teaching.

To say that I was feeling magnanimous at my twentieth high school reunion not long enough ago is, I suppose, an understatement. My ego was still basking in the afterglow of the writeup in the *New York Times*. United Press International had nicknamed me "the caped crusader of struggling superwomen." Capital "S" sacrifice your long-term well-being. You set your pace by monitoring your vitality. You know you are pushing too hard if you start to burn out; if you get bored, you aren't stretching enough.

There are many times when you are confused about what is next for you to do. Should you leave your safe, stale job to take the risk of starting your own company? Should you live off your life savings for a year to write a book? Should you pass up the promotion because you want to protect the time you have to spend with your family? Should you do this or do that?

Perhaps you have not considered the possibility that what is next for you to do is to sit in confusion for a while. When you are clear about what is next, answer the call. When you aren't, pause.

In the book *He: Understanding Masculine Philosophy* (Harper and Row, 1974), author Robert A. Johnson tells a classic story about the two great explorers of the inner realm, Carl Jung and Sigmund Freud. Soon after falling out with his mentor Freud, Jung found himself confused and upset. It took tremendous courage to break with Freud. Freud had the reputation and the track record. Jung was young, with little more than his convictions. He realized that this moment of uncertainty was a test of his beliefs: is the unconscious truly the fountain of creativity?

He locked himself in his room and waited. Before long, he was down on the floor playing children's games. He took his childhood fantasies into the backyard, building out of stone the villages, towns and forts he had imagined as a young boy. He trusted this process—

shined up for the occasion, I swept through the crowd, bestowing greetings to the little people of my class I remembered so well.

But the sweetest moment of my rapidly fading youth came when I saw, standing alone in the hallway, my nemesis from senior year. I couldn't help but notice that compared to me, in my opinion, he did not look good.

Back when we were budding journalists vying for editorship of the *New Trier News*, the competition between us was fierce. The publication board came up with what they thought would be an ideal solution: he and I would be named co-editors.

We were advised of the idea separately. Would I be willing to share the editorship?

Frankly, I could barely stand to be in the same room with the fellow. But being sweet sixteen and former All-Around Girl Scout to boot, I said, "Sure." My nemesis, when asked the same question, volunteered that if he were forced to share the job with me, he would quit.

When it finally came time for the banquet announcing the positions, parents, friends and fellow students gathered, breathlessly awaiting the news.

I lost. But even as the applause for my nemesis still rang in my ears, I knew I'd been launched into a greater destiny. I was innocence clenched in a battle with the dark side. I, the bearer of the standards for all that is virtuous, good and brave, was locked in an eternal dance with arrogance and greed. Somewhere, somehow, someday, fate would rectify this grave misstep.

Twenty years later, I faced him. He was not the force of mythic proportions I remembered. No, here was the shrunken wizard himself, emerging from behind memory's fearsome facade.

He'd seen the articles about me, he offered.

He was rumpled, slumped in the shoulders as he filled me in on his ups and downs of the intervening years. While I quietly basked in his seeming misfortunes, fate was at work behind the scenes, for both of us.

He told me he had been working on a novel for some time. He had no idea if it was any good or how it would be received.

I left the reunion feeling vindicated and restored, a painful chapter of my life come to its bittersweet conclusion.

Or so I thought.

For not long after my own book was published to a small (but fervent) following, his novel came out. Its title: *Presumed Innocent*. My nemesis: none other than the publishing industry's latest lion—Scott Turow.

Scott's book, substantiated by millions of dollars in hardcover, paperback and movie rights sales, is a brilliant tour de force, exposing with unprecedented candor the dark side of humanity. There is sex, there is murder, there is jealousy, greed and deception and every manner of evil.

With this book (and his subsequent *Burden of Proof*) on every rack in America, I have no place to hide from the inevitable ironies of fate. Ambition turned on me, for me, and on me again. Like a bug writhing on the pin of my own desire, I was forced—at last—to look beyond the moral rectification I felt I was owed by fate. Instead, I finally asked the question I had put off for over two decades.

What did Scott have that I wanted so badly? What did he have that I was missing?

When I explored this question in depth, I came to some startling realizations. It wasn't really the fame he had garnered. I had achieved my lifelong goal of making a guest appearance on *The Today Show*, discovering to my surprise that I felt less like the celebrated guest I'd fantasized myself to be and more like a product packaged into hard-selling sound-bites designed to make the commercials look good.

It wasn't really the money, either.

I finally admitted it was the sense that Scott could continue to romp comfortably in the dark side, while I sacrificed so much of myself—my honesty, my integrity, my authenticity—in order to be "good." It was I, after all, who had betrayed my authentic feelings by lying to the newspaper appointments board, I who had held so much of myself in abeyance, so many times in the many years since then, in order to live up to the glossy images I had constructed of myself sometime during my childhood.

What would a fuller expression of myself entail? What was it I really wanted to do?

My first indication of what this might look like came during an exploratory group art meditation. With the assignment to use the materials on hand to create a self-portrait of our spirits—rather than our appearances—the group quietly went to work. A ground-cloth had been spread out before us, stocked lavishly with yarns, feathers, beads and fur.

Determined to experiment with authenticity, I sat immobilized as I awaited inspiration. With good intentions to tune into my inner voice, I could not help but notice that several of the attendees had rushed the groundcloth, grabbing for the fluffiest yarns, shiniest beads and longest feathers. In the time it took to shut and open my eyes, all the pinks, purples, whites and yellows had been snapped up. What was left in the rapidly diminishing pile was a whole lot of black, red and brown. I was angry!

I'd paid a fair bit of change for this chance to learn to give fuller expression to my authenticity, and all I could think were the blackest thoughts. And then I realized how perfect this was. There was, after all, plenty of black in the pile. Wasn't my anger authentic, too?

I took some black yarn and began winding it around a webbed frame, a fierce center for my first foray into a more honest expression of myself. Out of the corner of my eye, I saw a gentle woman sew the finishing touches on her portrait: a dreamy blend of lovely pastels, glimmering like angel wings above the clouds.

I grabbed red out of the pile, to vent the anger and jealousy that welled up in me.

Back and forth I went, between red and black, black and red. And then, as the skein of dark passions I was working with came to an abrupt end, I realized that I was so inside the process of creation, my experience had transformed. In fact, a feeling of quiet joy had crept up in me when I was looking the other way. Magically, the woman with the pastel creation chose just that moment to return her excess materials to the groundcloth. I had the entire spectrum of colors and textures available to me, weaving the many moods and emotions that swirled through the process of my creation into my self-portrait. There were wild oranges, subtle peach and vibrant blues.

The process was wild and exciting—a synthesis of all that I am—the dark energies as well as the light-giving spirit. As it unfolded, I did not stop to think much about whether my object was pretty, whether it would meet with awe and approval. The few times I did, I threw that fear and desire into the vibrant assemblage as well. I used everything. I was ruthless. I was inspired!

The forces at play in our lives are so much greater than our limited perspectives can understand. We aim for perfection, but the lifeforce battles our efforts to contain and control, and bursts forth in creation. There is no safety in this, for the energy of the lifeforce is both creative and destructive. All there is is life, itself: chaotic, awake and alive. When we dig down to our core, we will not find a diamond sparkling in purity and innocence. The lifeforce is not a diamond: it is a hungry, birthing, chaotic, wild, burning, primal force.

At birth—enduring the narrow canal to burn our lungs with our first breath of air—we instinctively understand all of this. We each contain the memory of what it means to be fully alive. But the memory dims. As the third principle demonstrated, the process of growing up teaches us to surrender to the system to which we were born. We give up authentic expression for acceptance, continuing the sacrifice long after our survival is in question.

But it is that long-buried memory of being fully alive that continues to stir our discontent. The restlessness moves us to change careers again, buy bigger houses, try another child. We can stop now, giving up our quest for perfection to take up the greater challenge of giving ourselves permission to be what we already are.

I can forgive myself the arrogance of my youthful ambitions, understanding that the mistake was to think that it was my destiny alone to make an important contribution to the world. That destiny belongs to us all. And it does not come through our achievements alone, although achievement may be a by-product of the process. It is no less than the hero's journey, having the courage to confront the forces that conspire to deaden our spirits: the illusions, myths and erroneous beliefs.

In the tarot deck, there is a card called The Hermit. Alfred Douglas, in his book *The Tarot* (Penguin, 1972), describes him as "an old man who moves slowly along a dim and stony road. He is dressed in garments resembling those of a monk. The way before him is poorly lighted by a lantern which he carries in his right hand, shielded by his sleeve from the force of the wind."

He is the archetypal symbol of the quest for meaning. The way is lonely and he has only the light of his own intuition to help him find the right path.

"To essay such an adventure takes considerable courage," Douglas says, "for by abandoning conventional values in favor of the dictates of his inner self he is setting himself apart from the comforts and authority of society in order to follow a lonely road that leads he knows not where. The Hermit illustrates a crisis of will which must be met and overcome by anyone who would advance beyond the common pale."

The challenge of The Hermit is summarized in this quote by the philosopher Schopenhauer:

> Life may be compared to a piece of embroidery, of
> which, during the first half of his time, a man gets a sight
> of the right side, and during the second half, of the
> wrong. The wrong side is not so pretty as the right, but
> it is more instructive; it shows the way in which the
> threads have been worked together.

When you can come to appreciate the "wrong" side of the cloth from which you have woven your life, you will be inspired. If you are unaware of the capacity for inspiration in yourself, it is because you are looking for something grand. Inspiration is simple but pervasive. You will recognize your inspiration when you give yourself permission to accept yourself as you are. Bring compassion to the truth. And then use everything you've got.

It was another member of my high school class who brought this point home for me. Sylvia was a talented vocalist throughout her school years. Her parents had always loved opera, and were amazed and delighted that their little girl had the potential to develop into what they considered to be the star of the musical world: a coloratura soprano. When she hit junior high school, her parents paid for the best training available, and Sylvia began in earnest to pursue a career as a coloratura soprano.

But while her childhood memories of music and song were passionate, Sylvia's struggles after graduation to make singing her career came coupled with stress, effort and strain. It became apparent to her that she was considered a lightweight in the musical circles she longed to join. The harder she tried, the less seriously she was taken. After several years trying for a break, she gave up in frustration.

When I spent time with her at that reunion, she was doing bookkeeping in her husband's business. She loved her family life, but felt frustrated and guilty about the derailment of her career. She had given up singing entirely. The memories of rejection and failure were too painful. She feared that if she were to face those feelings head-on, she would disappear forever into an abyss of remorse and self-pity.

And yet, she noted with irony, she still scanned audition notes and news. One day, an announcement caught her eye. The community symphonic chorus was auditioning for vocalists. This was not a bid for the operatic stardom that had in childhood seemed her destiny. But she decided to call, feeling reasonably certain that they would not have any openings for a coloratura soprano.

When she phoned, the secretary who answered revealed that

she was correct in her assessment. They had all of the sopranos in the highest coloratura ranges they needed. But they did need someone who could provide the lower, richer ranges of the mezzo. Sylvia declined, explaining her background and training. Rather than accepting her demurrer, the secretary got the choir director on the line. They were in dire, immediate need for a mezzo — wouldn't she be willing to give it a try? The courageous voice that responded affirmatively was born of Sylvia's certainty that she would be eliminated on the spot. She could assuage her guilt about her aborted career without having to put anything important about herself on the line.

Thus defended, she arrived for her first audition in years. The accompaniest opened a simple piece from the mezzo repertoire before her and began playing. Sylvia's voice sounded thick. She threw her hands up and started to leave but the choir director stopped her. He urged her to try again.

She felt her face flush at the embarassment of not only this failure — but all her failures. The piano started up again. Struggling with the new terrain of the mezzo range, Sylvia began to cry. She stopped again.

This time the director said, even more firmly, "Keep singing." For several long minutes, she alternated between sobbing and singing as something inside her that she had long ago tamed turned wild again. Through the tears, it became apparent to all assembled that her voice was relaxing into the lower ranges with a richness and fullness she had not experienced in song since the unstructured days of her childhood, before the serious training began. Sylvia had always been a mezzo. There was where her strength and power lay. She was anything but a lightweight in the middle ranges. She was offered the job on the spot.

Before every performance, she takes a moment to remember. It wasn't just the discovery of her true range that freed her authentic voice, Sylvia humbly reminds herself. It was her willingness not only to sing despite her pain, her failure and her insecurity, but to sing with her pain, her failure and her insecurity—to give expression to all of her life experiences.

The Sufi tradition has simple wisdom to guide us: trust and allow your doing to become a prayer.

It is possible for you not to trust the universe, and still be doing. This is, in fact, the destructive nature of our contemporary business environment. You can also trust the universe and be lazy. But if you trust the universe and remain a doer, you will be an instrument of the lifeforce. Your process will be the process of the lifeforce. Your manifestations and results will be no less than lifeforce manifesting through you.

Principle Number Seven

To achieve greatness, you must be willing to surrender ambition.

CONCLUSION

Forgive your limitations
and get on with your life.

WHEN WE LEFT Sylvia, she had just been offered a job as a mezzo soprano in the orchestra choir. What do you think happened next?

A. She accepted the job and soon distinguished herself as one of the finest mezzo sopranos in the history of that orchestra. Before long, she was receiving invitations to solo with orchestras around the state. When we last spoke, she had just been offered the starring role in the fall opera season.

B. She accepted the job and enjoyed singing in the choir very much. But she hadn't taken into account the rigorous rehearsal and performance schedules. She found herself missing the time she had been spending working side by side with her husband, and the flexibility and freedom of being with her children at her own discretion. Performing with the chorus for one season was a completion for her—acknowledgment of who she was at her deepest level. She was able to leave her career at last, without remorse and regret. In addition to returning to her job as bookkeeper to her husband, she joined the church choir—as a mezzo.

C. She loved being in the choir. While she was rarely chosen for solos, she turned out to be a strong team player. She got great joy and satisfaction sharing her life experiences with younger choir members, coming to enjoy her role as mentor just as much as her job as vocalist.

The answer you guessed—be it A, B or C—will tell you more about yourself than it will about Sylvia. For when we last spoke, any of the above were distinct possibilities. Sylvia had accepted the position and in short order had descended from elation to confusion. There were things she loved about her new life, and things she missed. There were opportunities opening up, but there were costs. The same willingness to experience all of her feelings that helped Sylvia land the job served her through this transition. She was not afraid of confusion. In fact, on some level, she had to admit that she enjoyed not knowing everything for a change. She could hang out patiently with irresolution, feeling her way through to whatever would be next. Inspired by the lifeforce she felt manifesting, she trusted that she was being guided to the fulfillment of her destiny.

Do you hope that Sylvia becomes a big star? She took a risk making the internal leap to the vulnerability she brought to her audition. Is her reward riches, glory and fame? Is this how you will know that Sylvia is a success? Is this how you would know, for yourself, that you've "arrived"?

At this point, Sylvia is more involved with the discovery of her capacity to accept all the previously hidden parts of herself than with the need to hear applause. She is not thinking about whether she is "successful" or not. She is living her life fully.

This reminds me of advice given to me by a limousine driver, hired by my first publisher to shepherd me through a demanding day of interviews with the media in New York City. Afraid I was blowing it, forgetting to plug my book, missing opportunities to make clever points, I felt my television makeup running down my cheeks in big, black streaks.

The driver, an elderly man who ate a salami sandwich curbside during my appearances, looked at me crumpled in the back seat. He's seen them all, he commented, and they are all the same.

"They?" I understood, unfortunately, that the "they" he was talking about included me.

"You all come here, thinking you're going to swallow this city whole. Why? It's full of snakes. You want a belly full of snakes? You want my advice? When you're living with snakes, be a snake. Take your best bite fast—and get the hell out."

The salami lingered in the air as I pondered this. And then, from some miraculous source in my soul—far beyond the reaches of my personality—I realized that this was very, very funny.

In my own way, I have taken his sage advice. I am no longer trying to save the world and be recognized for it. Instead, inspired by the personal philosophy of the writer Isaac Asimov, I add my two cents when and where I can. If I can counterbalance even one moment of craziness with a little common sense, I figure I've done well for the day.

When you do achieve high levels of success, it is tempting to become overidentified with your product. For some, performing at your job may be the only place you feel alive. Is this inspiration or addiction? If you're not sure, see what happens when you try to take a break.

Do you spend your vacations breaking out in cold sweats about what you are missing at the office? Are you secretly thrilled at night or on the weekend when the phone rings and it's an emergency at work you simply must respond to? Is work the only place you feel alive?

You think you have courage exploring the outer bounds of human potential, becoming a master of the universe on the job. But do you have the courage not to act? To be in transition? To discover what it means to be not just on fire with work—but with life? How are your personal relationships? Can you hang out with family and friends without worrying that everything might not go as planned? What if it rains on your picnic or your new boyfriend hates your egg salad?

How is your relationship to yourself? Can you survive failure and not turn against others or yourself?

These principles do not ask you simply to move your addiction from your career to your family, or from your family to your self-improvement, or from your self-improvement to your spirituality.

As you recover the health of your internal systems--balancing overachievement and overinvestment with perspective and acceptance—your ability to manage your careers and businesses will recover as well. You will no longer need to throw ambition to anxiety like a bone to a demanding dog. You will no longer fear the revelation of the inevitable inadequacy you have secretly harbored, and so you can no longer be held the emotional hostage of bosses, clients or subordinates. You no longer give more than you could possibly get back, so you are freed from resentment.

You can work less and achieve more. But there's a big difference between the recovery from overinvestment, and the notion that if you follow your inspiration, you will be rewarded with money, fame and recognition.

In our society, vision has been confused with the belief that if we do what we love, money and success will follow. We have been taught to equate the fulfillment of our vision with success in the business arena. We think of the goal of success as living in comfort. For some of us, the two may coincide. But the truth is that for many of us, carrying out our vision may require sacrifices.

One day, not long ago, a poet turned to her wise aunt, sharing a painful moment. For years, she had poured her heart into a book of poems that had just been rejected for the twentieth time.

"I thought that if you courageously peel away the facade and take big risks by expressing your authentic self openly, the money will come."

Her aunt quietly poured another cup of lemonade.

"Dear niece," she said, "it is more likely to turn out that way when you peel down to the core and find that your authentic self contains an investment banker inside."

You get into difficulty when you confuse your potential to have unlimited vision with the childlike belief that you have unlimited means, as well. You find acceptance when you realize that your means will always be limited.

You have more brains but somebody else has family connections. He has family money but lacks your creative spunk. He has neurotic drives born from abusive neglect in the way he was parented. Who will garner the greater success in life? Who is likely to make more money? Who will achieve greater fulfillment?

Each of us has those things in our past and our makeup that work for us and against us. But as psychologist Rollo May points out in his book *Freedom and Destiny* (Norton, 1981), devoid of limitation, we would be like a river without banks. Without boundaries, we could never build sufficient velocity to move forward. Our genetic, historic, emotional and spiritual legacies propel us through our lives. We can thrash about in the currents, or catch the curl and hang ten.

Perhaps doing what's next will bring us to a time and place that calls for heroism on a grand public scale. Perhaps our moment of heroism is quiet and internal. It is vision enough to find as much time in our lives as we can muster to love our children, our spouses, our friends; or to create for the sheer ecstasy of self-expression; or to take joy in the growth of our character through challenge and adversity.

So what if our jobs do not supply us with the outlet for creative expression, social life, meaningful contribution and sufficient money to impress our friends? The search for the rewards we have been taught that we deserve for our good behavior has taken us from position to position, job to job, career to career.

But no boss, no work environment, no career can fill the emptiness where the universe's end of the bargain—the promise that if we were good enough we could have it all—was supposed to be.

When we embark upon the path to life-driven careers and businesses, we stop wasting energy trying to make business perform at the behest of our childish fantasies. Instead, we are grateful for what work does do: provide us with the means to support our lives. Because you know you have a roof over your head and food on the table, you can, if you so choose, be among the privileged few on this planet who can move beyond issues of personal survival and begin to explore expanded dimensions of the potential to be more fully alive.

You don't need to throw away everything you've worked for. There is no guarantee that giving away all your possessions and going to sit on a mountaintop deep in meditation will take you to peace and fulfillment any faster than staying in your old job, taking the time to bring an expanded awareness and perspective to it.

Rabbi Nathan Segal told his Marin County congregation the story of a seeker of wisdom. He had heard of a spiritual master who had spent years atop a sacred mountain. The seeker had heard that this master had discovered the secret to happiness.

The seeker set out to find this master, risking his life to cross frozen fields of snow, climb barren foothills, hang from cliffs — finally to arrive at the master's feet.

"Master! I have come all this way. Tell me. What is the secret of happiness?"

The master took a deep breath and then stated:

"It's the sunset."

"The sunset?" the seeker asked incredulously.

The master paused a moment then responded.

"It's not the sunset?"

We all have security needs. There is a healthy balance between security and risk that will be unique to you. The experience of being fully alive is yours alone — given who you are, where you've come from, where you are in your personal process. You don't have to take every risk. But are you willing to do what's next? Nobody outside yourself can judge how well you are doing. Forgive yourself and forgive your career and your business for its limitations and get on with your life.

When you give up resentment, even simple tasks can hold great fulfillment. A Zen master, encountering a teacher putting the finishing touches on a remodeled kitchen at the Zen Center, asked how things were going.

"Everything's going fine," the teacher answered. "There are only a few details to finish up."

Upon hearing this, the master scratched his head.

"Only a few details? But details are all there are."

You are afraid your status in life does not reflect your full potential? Work, no matter how mundane, can provide an opportunity to be of service to our great visions. We can practice teamwork, compassion, discipline and responsiveness—even if the task we are doing is cleaning the house.

Ironically, at the very moment we stop demanding our careers to deliver success to us, we find ourselves attracting to us those who want what we now have: the ability to operate out of support of life, not out of fear. Those who were previously able to engage us in their reward and punishment-driven games of power, fall away. When our spirit is strong, we repel those who once fed off our denial. We stop taking abuse from clients, bosses and subordinates and start to demand respect . . . and we stop passing the abuse along.

If, as a result, we are in a position to take a new job, or to hire a new employee, we can seek out people to work with who complement not only our skills but our visions. The strength and

stability of our companies reflect the degree to which we can support each other to bring our values and our spirits to work with us
each day.

The work of transforming our experience of business from fear
to life begins with these principles. But the internal work prescribed in this book is only the beginning. Over the coming
decade, as managers develop sufficient inner strength, the
overflow will transform our corporate environment. Released from
the carrot and the stick, few of us will want to continue the sixty-
or seventy-hour weeks that have become the norm.

When we work to live, rather than live to work, we realize that
should we choose to limit ourselves to forty hours of work a week,
we can leave enough time for us to nurture other important
aspects of our lives. When we give ourselves time to refresh and
revitalize, we return to work with our entire capacity to produce
renewed and available.

The creative options for cultivating and revitalizing ourselves and
our subordinates are as unlimited as the human imagination: from
flex-time to increased vacations; from allowing time for reflection
in the workday without reprimand, to cutting out overtime.

An increasing number of companies are experimenting with
new ways of working for both men and women that take into con-
sideration the whole person's needs and values through all life
stages: on-site daycare; maternity and paternity leaves; sabbati-
cals. Beyond these logistical adjustments, there are the attendant
changes in attitude prescribed by these principles. In the age of

the global economy, coupled with dramatic demographic shifts, the corporation of the future will need leaders who can work interpersonally with employees of many cultures, ages and educational backgrounds. The challenges of the future will cause managers to call upon inner resources as never before. Those who will have the competitive advantage are the very people who have taken the time to do the difficult internal work prescribed in this book. The external and the internal will converge in the simple realization destined to change the way we do business in this country: life-driven people build life-driven businesses.

We are pioneers poised on the brink of yet another frontier: the human spirit. An account supervisor at an advertising agency in San Francisco is one such explorer. Landing a major baby food company as a client, he was quick to let his staff know that "there would be no room for mistakes." He never took vacations, working nights and weekends "in case something came up."

He read everything pertaining to his industry and kept abreast of all related information. A single man, too busy to initiate ongoing intimate relationships, he rarely ventured outside his office or apartment. On the rare occasion he did, he grilled the children of neighbors and friends for additional data on food preferences. He was hooked on power and control—but the price was enormous.

Staff turnover was a big problem. But the bigger problem was that constantly going on overdrive, he was forced to do everything the hard and long way. He was cut off from inspiration and creativity. As long as things went well, he was in great form. But when things didn't go exactly the way he wanted, he could not regain equilibrium without the benefit of increasingly large glasses of wine. Devoid of perspective, his long hours soothed by alcohol seemed perfectly reasonable to him. Before long, his dependence on drinking was out of control. The man who never wanted to leave anything to chance was ultimately forced to take an extended leave of absence at a dependency treatment center.

While there, he was forced to flow with the ebbs and tides of his recovery. Ironically, in his absence, his division experienced a similar release. His staff, freed from the frenetic, fear-driven pace, began producing out of spontaneous creativity. Upon his return, recognizing that the division had not fallen apart in his absence, the executive vowed to continue to watch his pacing—and to acknowledge and honor his need for balance in his life.

Within a year, his division transformed into one of the healthiest in the company; and he surprised everybody, including himself, by falling in love and marrying a woman with two young sons. Several years later, the happiest he has ever been, he observes that the more he had surrendered control, the more his division and life thrived.

When asked his secret to working less and achieving more, he gave credit to a Twelve Step Program prayer he had learned in recovery.

"God, here I am and here are all my troubles. I've made a
mess of things and can't do anything about it. You take me,
and all of my troubles, and do anything you want with me."

When you commit yourself to telling the truth, trusting that you are responsible enough to yourself to hold whatever you discover with acceptance and compassion, you will flow into what's next for you. You won't need to push or control the outcome. You will sacrifice the illusion that you can bribe fate with your good behavior—but you will receive, in return, the gift of partnership with the lifeforce.

Trusting that larger forces than yourself are at work in your life, you will give up the demand for the outcome you think you want and learn to appreciate whatever it is you get. This is true freedom.

The challenge of our generation of leadership is to cut through the tyranny of the illusion of control and expand our definition of success to include spiritual qualities and life experiences that run counter to virtually every precept of contemporary American business philosophy. The irony is that by doing what seems diametrically opposed to all our notions of what it takes to succeed, we find the only path that leads to an experience of success that can endure.

There is a Persian story about a young man who stumbled upon a mountain cave. Peering cautiously inside, he spied a priceless pearl clasped in the claws of a fierce dragon. The boy plotted and planned, but eventually gave up trying to retrieve the pearl. He reconciled himself to living an ordinary life.

Over the years, he got a job. He married and had children. He lived his life, forgetting about the pearl until he was very old. Then one day, he remembered.

Taking up his walking stick, he hobbled to the cave. To his amazement, the pearl was still there. But even more astonishing, the dragon had shrunk to the size of a harmless lizard. The old man easily picked up the pearl and carried it away. The fierce battle that he'd plotted in his youth had been fought inside himself as he met the challenges of his daily life. It was not really the dragon that had diminished. It was he who had grown in inner strength and stature.

We can redefine success for ourselves, experiencing fulfillment whatever the "facts" of our careers appear to be at any given time. We can replace ambition with purpose, fueling our actions by inspiration rather than fear. Ultimately, as my company did, we can reap the benefits of working less and achieving more.

On the path prescribed in *Inner Excellence*, there are no dead-ends, no wrong turns. You are fulfilling your purpose the most direct way possible–regardless of your apparent results at the time. You don't know what to do next? Begin anywhere. When you begin to act, the action changes you as you find resources inside of you that you did not know you had.

These seven principles worked for me. I have faith they will work for you.

THE SEVEN PRINCIPLES
OF LIFE-DRIVEN BUSINESS

1. Change your beliefs about the nature of business and of life, and you will change how you manage your career.
2. In order to become fully successful, you must first be fully alive.
3. When you empty yourself of the illusions of who and what you think you are, there is less to lose than you had feared.
4. You have the choice between being the victim of circumstances or being empowered through them.
5. When you are driven by life, the odds will be with you.
6. Your ordinary self is enough.
7. To achieve greatness, you must be willing to surrender ambition.

May you find the courage to persist gently over time.

TAKING THE NEXT STEP TOGETHER

I F YOU would like to be on the Inner Excellence mailing list, to be informed of talks by Carol Orsborn in your city or upcoming plans for consulting, seminars and training programs; or if you would like to subscribe to "Inner Excellence: The Bulletin of Business and Spirituality," please write to Inner Excellence, 1766 Union Street, Suite C, San Francisco, CA 94123. A year's subscription to the quarterly newsletter is $67.

If you would like to put together a support group on the principles presented in this book, you might want to consider the following format:

Take turns leading a weekly meeting. The session leader begins by reading a short portion of this book or any pre-selected offering drawn from books on the source list, or any favorite inspirational book suggesting the theme for discussion.

Following the reading, a member of the group takes a few minutes to respond, based on the career or business challenges he or she is facing. The first respondent concludes, and calls on the next person who wishes to speak. Resist the urge to offer advice or engage in cross-conversation during this portion of the meeting so that as many individuals as possible can have a turn.

After everyone who wishes to has participated (or after a predetermined period of time), each person makes the following statement to the group: "I ask the group to support me this week. What I really want is _____."

Each person states, as succinctly as possible, a specific goal, such as "less stress," "to hire a supportive secretary," "more energy," and so on. After each person makes a request, the group responds, "I support you in this." There can be general discussion following, as time allows.

At the conclusion, next week's leader is selected. This is followed by reading aloud the "Prayer for Life-Driven Business" on page 99 of this book.

This format is only a suggestion. If you want to start a group and would like assistance connecting with others, please let me know and I will announce the group's formation in my bulletin.

APPENDIX A:
ADDITIONAL STATISTICAL SUPPORT

K EY FINDINGS: Northwestern National Life Insurance Company study "Employee Burnout: America's Newest Epidemic," copyrighted 1991. The research, conducted among 600 full-time employees nationwide, including both blue-collar and white-collar workers, is reprinted with permission of Northwestern National Life Insurance.

- One in three Americans seriously thought about quitting work in 1990 because of job stress, and one in three expects to "burn out" on the job in the near future. Fourteen percent quit or changed jobs in the past two years due to job stress.
- Stress levels are extremely or very high for nearly half of the respondents. One in three say job stress is the single greatest stress in their lives.

- Seven of 10 workers say job stress lowers their productivity, and they experience frequent health ailments. It also causes them to miss one or more days of work a year.
- Seventy-two percent of all workers experience three or more stress-related illnesses somewhat or very often; 62% of American workers report that they often experience exhaustion; 62% also report that they often experience muscle pain; 45% report that they often get headaches; and 45% report that they often experience the inability to sleep. Other stress-related illnesses often experienced by at least one-third of those reporting: depression, ulcers or intestinal disorders, respiratory illness.
- The occurrence of stress-related disabilities is increasing. Based on the number of disability cases managed in NWNL rehabilitation services, the proportion of stress-related disabilities has doubled over the last nine years from 6 to 13 percent.
- Rehabilitating workers suffering from stress-related disabilities is more difficult than rehabilitating disabilities overall. Success rates for rehabilitating stress-related disabilities averaged 50 percent while success rates overall have remained at about 75 percent.

APPENDIX B:
INSPIRING SOURCES

MANY TEACHERS have helped me in developing these ideas—individuals with whom I have been privileged to study in person as well as many authors and philosophical systems that have guided my journey in writing. While I have not always agreed with everything they have shared with me, I have always learned from them. I have listed here some of my most inspiring sources.

Alcoholics Anonymous. *Alcoholics Anonymous*. Alcoholics Anonymous World Services, Inc., 1987.

Bill B. *Compulsive Overeater*. CompCare Publications, 1981.

Blum, Ralph. *The Book of Runes*. St. Martin's Press, 1987.

Boland, Jack. *Master Mind Goal Achiever's Journal*. Master Mind Publishing Company, 1990.

Campbell, Joseph, with Bill Moyers. *The Power of Myth*. Doubleday, 1988.

The Dalai Lama. *A Policy of Kindness*. Snow Lion Publications, 1990.

Douglas, Alfred. *The Tarot*. Penguin, 1972.

Douglas, Nik and Penny Slinger. *The Secret Dakini Oracle*. Destiny Books, 1979.

Emery, Stewart. *The Owner's Manual for Your Life*. Doubleday, 1982.

Fields, Rick. *Chop Wood Carry Water: A Guide to Finding Spiritual Fulfillment in Everyday Life*. Tarcher, 1984.

Harman, Willis, Ph.D. *Global Mind Change*. Knowledge Systems, Inc., The Institute for Noetic Sciences, 1988.

Huffines, LaUna. *Connecting with All the People in Your Life*. Harper and Row, 1986.

Johnson, Robert A. *He: Understanding Masculine Psychology*. Harper and Row, 1974.

Johnson, Warren. *Muddling Toward Frugality: A Blueprint for Survival in the 1980's*. Shambhala, 1979.

Kushner, Harold. *Who Needs God*. Pocket Books, 1989.

Levinson, Daniel J. *The Seasons of a Man's Life*. Ballantine Books, 1978.

May, Rollo. *Freedom and Destiny*. W.W. Norton, 1981.

Muktananda. *Where are You Going? A Guide to the Spiritual Journey*. Gurudev Siddha Peeth, 1981.

Muktananda. *Play of Consciousness*. Syda Foundation, 1978.

Phillips, Dorothy Berkley. *The Choice is Always Ours*. Family Library, 1974.

Rajneesh. *Neo-Tarot*. Rajneesh Foundation International, 1983.

Rifkin, Jeremy. *Time Wars: The Primary Conflict in Human History*. Touchstone, 1987.

Shames, Laurence. *The Hunger for More: Searching for Values in an Age of Greed*. Times Books, 1989.

Shi, David E. *The Simple Life: Plain Living and High Thinking in American Culture*. Oxford, 1985.

Shield, Benjamin and Richard Carlson, Ph.D. *For the Love of God: New Writings By Spiritual and Psychological Leaders*. New World Library, 1990.

Smith, LaGard F. *Out on a Broken Limb*. Harvest House Publishers, 1986.

Stone, Hal Ph.D. and Sidra Winkelman, Ph.D. *Embracing Ourselves*. New World Library, 1989.

Ueland, Brenda. *If You Want to Write: A Book About Art, Independence and Spirit*. Graywolf Press, 1987.

Walker, Barbara G. *The Crone: Woman of Age, Wisdom and Power*. HarperCollins, 1985.

Watts, Alan W. *The Spirit of Zen: A Way of Life, Work and Art in the Far East*. Grove Press, 1958.

Wilhelm, Richard (translator) and Cary F. Baynes. *The I Ching*. Foreward by Carl Jung. Princeton University Press, 1950.

Also by Carol Orsborn

Inner Excellence audio cassette   Price: $16.95
   2 cassettes   90 minutes

Enough is Enough:
Simple Solutions for Complex People   Price: $10.95

The groundbreaking book that first defined downward mobility is now available with a new introduction by the author. Orsborn shares her own struggle for balance in her hectic life, and shows how her choice of values over success led to greater personal satisfaction and fulfillment. It means learning to think in terms of having enough, not having more than enough, and learning to choose what you really want, rather than what others say you should have.

You need this book! —ERMA BOMBECK

Orsborn keeps us chuckling along with a variety of humorous anecdotes, but watch out—she is as angry as she is ebullient, as incisive and controversial as she is refreshing and funny. —SAN FRANCISCO CHRONICLE

Available at your local bookstore
Or send check or money order for $16.95* for each cassette, $10.95* for each book, plus $2.75 for shipping and handling for the first item, 50 cents for each additional item, along with your name and address, to:

New World Library
58 Paul Drive • San Rafael, CA 94903
Phone: (415) 472-2100 • FAX: (415) 472-6131
Or call toll free: (800) 227-3900 • In CA: (800) 632-2122

New World Library is dedicated to publishing books and cassettes that help improve the quality of our lives. For a catalog, please contact us at the above address.

* CA residents add applicable sales tax.

[150]